Praise for *The Course Sylla~~~~~~ ~~~~~~~~~~

"I can't imagine how many times I've recommended this book—to new faculty, to part-time teachers, to experienced pedagogues, and to faculty finding their way to more learner-centered approaches. I can't imagine a book more deserving of a second edition. And, I can't imagine a second edition better than the first, but this one is, thanks to the able efforts of two new authors." —Maryellen Weimer, professor emeritus, Penn State, and editor, the *Teaching Professor*

• • •

"New and veteran college teachers alike, in all types of institutions from the community college to the university level, will benefit from this highly thoughtful, scholarly, and persuasive argument for the critical role of the learning-centered course syllabus. The authors clearly and convincingly demonstrate how to create a learning-centered course syllabus that becomes a dynamic, essential part of a course that encourages student engagement, active learning, and critical thinking. A must-read for anyone committed to teaching today's college students to maximize their skills and knowledge for a changing world!" —Angela Provitera McGlynn, professor emeritus of psychology and author of *Teaching Today's College Students* and *Successful Beginnings for College Teaching*

• • •

"It's obvious that Millis and Cohen have extensive backgrounds in college teaching and learning. Their work on the syllabus as a fundamental component of good teaching is supportive, insightful, current, and practical. This is a masterful updating of Grunert's classic, relevant across all disciplines." —Nancy Chism, professor of higher education, Indiana University

• • •

The Course Syllabus

A Learning-Centered Approach

Second Edition

**Judith Grunert O'Brien,
Barbara J. Millis,
Margaret W. Cohen**
Foreword by Robert M. Diamond

JOSSEY-BASS
A Wiley Imprint
www.josseybass.com

Contents

Foreword   xi

Preface   xiii

Acknowledgments   xvii

The Authors   xix

PART I: FOCUS ON LEARNING

Preparing Students   3

Setting a Framework for Knowledge   4

Planning Your Learning-Centered Syllabus: An Overview
of the Process   13

Composing a Learning-Centered Syllabus   21

Using a Learning-Centered Syllabus   34

PART II: EXAMPLES

Checklist   39

Table of Contents   40

Instructor Information   41

Student Information Form   43

Letter to the Students or Teaching Philosophy Statement   44

Purpose of the Course   49

Course Description   51

Course Objectives   54

Readings   63

Resources   65

Course Calendar   67

Course Requirements   71

Policies and Expectations: Attendance, Late Papers,
Missed Tests, Class Behaviors, and Civility   77

Policies and Expectations: Academic Integrity, Disability
Access, and Safety   87

Evaluation   92

Grading Procedures   98

How to Succeed in the Course: Tools for Study and Learning   102

PART III: SUGGESTED READINGS

General Teaching   111

Active Learning   112

Assessment and Evaluation   113

Cooperative and Collaborative Learning   113

Course and Curriculum Design   114

Critical Thinking   115

Information Technology   115

Learning and Motivation   116

Student Differences   116

Online Resources for Syllabus Construction   118

Teaching Portfolios   118

References   121

Index   127

This book is dedicated to our college
and university colleagues who are teaching students
to value the processes of learning as much as they do.

Foreword

THE RESEARCH ON teaching and learning is consistent: the more information you provide your students about the goals of a course, their responsibilities, and the criteria you will use to evaluate their performance, the more successful they will be as students and the more successful you will be as a teacher. This is no easy task. It requires a great deal of effort on your part and, often, far more work than you originally anticipate.

The first step is to develop a clear set of learning goals or outcomes for each course and for every one of its units. You will then want to ensure that the methods you use to evaluate student success align with the goals of these courses. In addition, students need to understand—and perceive as fair—the criteria you will use to determine their grades and the standards of acceptable performance. After you have determined the goals and the evaluation criteria, you can then focus on the specific activities and assignments that will help students achieve the goals. Students will also need to know what you expect of them academically and socially. Perhaps equally challenging, students must read and use this information once you provide it to them.

Unfortunately, in too many instances your students will enter your course without the study skills and habits necessary to effectively use even the best information. Today's students need you to reinforce the importance of the material you provide and give them detailed information on how to best use it. Just handing students a quality study guide or syllabus is not enough. You need to introduce the importance of your stated learning goals, show students how these outcome statements are directly related to how they are evaluated, and then reinforce this relationship through quizzes, tests, and assignments early and often.

In addition, technology, changing demographics, distance education, and new ways of thinking about the nature of knowledge in the information age have prompted many changes in teaching that may be unfamiliar to your students. New learning opportunities abound through the Internet, including Web sites (such as MySpace and YouTube), e-mail, and course management systems (such as Blackboard, WebCampus, Angel, and Moodle)—which all allow academic exchanges to occur outside regular class meetings. The significant increase in part-time and adult students (including first-generation students), as well as in internships and extended classroom activities, has affected the nature of what and how we teach. The traditional one- to three-page syllabus is ineffective for helping students understand their expanding role in the learning enterprise. To understand the expectations that you have of them and the plans that have been established for their learning experience, your students need more comprehensive information than the traditional syllabus provides. *The Course Syllabus: A Learning-Centered Approach* addresses student learning and responds to this question: what do students need to know to derive maximum benefit from their educational experience?

Many faculty have already gone far beyond the shorter syllabus. John Lough (1997), in a study of Carnegie Professor of the Year award winners, found important similarities in syllabi designed by these exemplary teachers. Most obvious was the detailed precision. Each contained clearly stated course objectives; a day-by-day schedule identifying specific reading assignments and due dates; and clear statements regarding make-up dates, attendance, and grading standards. These syllabi also provided students with the times when the professor would be available in the office, by e-mail, and by phone at home. Lough observed, "One gets the very clear impression that the Carnegie award winners have extraordinary expectations for their own behavior in and out of the classroom. Perhaps it is not so surprising, therefore, that these professors might impose some of these same standards on the students with whom they share so much." These high standards are manifest by what such teachers do in the classroom and by what they say in their syllabi.

Robert M. Diamond
Author of *Designing and Assessing Courses and Curricula*

Preface

MYRIAD CHALLENGES FACE American colleges and universities today, including serving an increasingly diverse student population and responding to the demands of an information society that is transforming the way we live, work, and learn. This diversity is reflected in how our students select campuses, choose majors, and enroll in courses. Some students base their choices on traditional factors—prestige, financial aid, legacy, program options, reputation—and others base their choices on mundane factors, such as convenience, proximity, and cost. More and more students are delaying college matriculation or going to school part-time. Many are fulfilling dreams to enroll in college after raising families or serving their country. They select courses that synchronize smoothly with their work and family schedules. They are first- and second-generation Americans. They are fluent in more than one language, or they may be learning to speak, read, and write in English as a second language. They travel around the world to attend a college in the United States, and they matriculate from the neighborhoods adjacent to our campuses. The diversity of our students increases the complexity of our instructional lives. Whether they're in a small seminar or a large lecture hall, our students bring to the classroom different knowledge sets and experiences, different reasons for pursuing degrees, different interests and motives, and different resources and skills for learning.

How do we respond to this heterogeneity? A renewed focus on student learning is one way of meeting these attitudinal and behavioral challenges. A first step is making a habit of applying our inquiry skills to our teaching and asking persistently, "How do I know my students are learning?" and "What's best for student learning?" Fortunately, we can rely on the extensive research on learning and motivation and consider which learning goals and teaching priorities will ensure that our students learn in meaningful, purposeful, and effective ways. Listening and watching for answers to questions like "How do I know my students understand this abstraction?" "How do I know everyone can replicate the problem solution?" and "How can I be certain that we've clarified misconceptions?" can help us focus creatively on the strategies that will steer the diverse learners in our classes to valuing academic success.

This guide frames the process of developing a comprehensive student syllabus as a reflective exercise that will lead to course improvement. Composing a syllabus that is centered on student learning is a challenging undertaking that requires substantial reflection and analysis. A learning-centered syllabus requires that you shift from what you, the instructor, are going to cover in your course to a concern for what information, tools, assignments, and activities you can provide to promote your students' learning and intellectual development. It is an evolving process that is enhanced by repeated opportunities to teach the same course to different learners.

Your syllabus represents a significant point of interaction, often the first, between you and your students. When thoughtfully prepared, your syllabus will demonstrate the interplay of your understanding of students' needs and interests, your beliefs and assumptions about the nature of learning and education, and your values and interests concerning course content and structure. When carefully designed, your syllabus will provide your students with essential information and resources that can help them become effective learners by actively shaping their own learning. It will minimize misunderstandings by providing you and your students with a common plan and set of references.

Organization

Part I of this book reflects on the implications of the learning context and adopting a focus on learning for you and your students. We hope it guides you to discover fresh insights and new ways to develop a course syllabus. Included are sections on planning a learning-centered syllabus, composing it to serve a number of functions, and using it as a learning tool throughout a course. In each section, we call attention to integrating various technologies, especially course management systems, to enhance the form, function, and use of the syllabus.

Part II offers excerpts from syllabi developed for courses in many disciplines at colleges and universities across the United States. These examples may not necessarily have been developed within a framework of learning-centeredness, but they all contribute something to this perspective. Each was recommended by faculty developers who are well attuned to learning-centered teaching. Since we routinely do not exchange syllabi with one another, reviewing these examples will offer new ideas for content and style and will affirm some of the risks you may have taken already as you developed and updated syllabi for your courses. Learning how others construct objectives, phrase expectations, convey a course policy, or design an assignment may be the encouragement many of us need to redesign part of our syllabus or course or to try an innovation.

Part III includes an annotated list of suggested readings that you will find useful for further exploration of issues raised in this guide. The topics include general teaching, active learning, assessment and evaluation, cooperative and collaborative learning, course and curriculum design, critical thinking, information technology, learning and motivation, student differences, online resources for constructing a syllabus, and references to develop an annotated teaching portfolio that you can use to document innovations and improvements in your teaching.

Benefits to Instructors

As the instructor responsible for teaching a course, you are usually responsible for developing course materials, starting with a course syllabus. This book will help you. By thinking through course goals, assessment and grading practices, course content, and student activities, you will confront issues of consistency and practicality. These considerations will lead to a more carefully designed course, one that consistently focuses on your students and their learning.

A learning-centered syllabus can help reinforce the roles that you expect students to take in your course. By providing concrete descriptions of tools and procedures, you will be prepared to help those students who may be unfamiliar or uncomfortable with active and collaborative learning approaches.

While this guide was developed with college and university instructors in mind, it should also be useful to others, including:

- Faculty mentors of junior faculty, new faculty, and TAs
- Department chairs, program directors, and deans
- Administrators of academic affairs
- Members of curriculum committees

- Accreditation planning teams
- Faculty development specialists
- Instructional designers
- Students of educational practice
- Other postsecondary educators

Transforming your courses into the kinds of educational environments where students share responsibility for shaping their learning is an evolving process, for you as well as for your students. Developing a learning-centered syllabus can compel you and your colleagues to clarify curricular goals and instructional priorities and to discuss how to promote learning in a discipline or across a program.

Barbara Millis
Excellence in Teaching Program
University of Nevada, Reno

Margaret Cohen
Center for Teaching and Learning
University of Missouri–St. Louis

Acknowledgments

WE WISH TO thank Judith Grunert O'Brien for her foresight and inspiring work on the first edition of this text. We also are grateful to our many colleagues in the Professional and Organizational Development Network in Higher Education who sent us stimulating syllabi from creative faculty on their own campuses. We especially want to thank the contributors themselves, who offered their work and whose carefully constructed syllabi provide the examples and tested applications that will help others make the connections with students that are so important for learning.

Special thanks go to Karolina Urbanowska, a talented graduate student in the Excellence for Teaching Program at the University of Nevada, Reno. She pitched in eagerly and competently to end hours of frustration over the formatting of the book and the copyright permissions. At the University of Missouri–St. Louis, immeasurable help was received from Cheryl Bielema, Cheryle Cann, and Vicki Lock. At home, we thank our families for respecting our obsessions and the project and for finding fitting ways to support us.

Barbara Millis
Margaret Cohen

The Authors

JUDITH GRUNERT O'BRIEN, the original author, was a member of the School of Art faculty at Syracuse University's College of Visual and Performing Arts when she wrote the first edition of *The Course Syllabus: A Learning-Centered Approach* in 1997.

BARBARA J. MILLIS, who received her PhD in English literature from Florida State University, has been active in faculty development since 1982, when she became the staff development specialist for the University of Maryland University College's Asian Division. She works with faculty around the globe on course redesign, active and cooperative learning, peer review (including classroom observations), classroom assessment techniques, academic games, and so forth. She heads the Excellence in Teaching Program at the University of Nevada, Reno.

MARGARET W. COHEN is the associate provost for professional development and founding director of the Center for Teaching and Learning at the University of Missouri–St. Louis. She joined the UM–St. Louis faculty in 1980 and chaired the Division of Educational Psychology, Research and Evaluation in the College of Education before adding her current responsibilities in the Office of Academic Affairs in 2000. She designs campus programs for faculty, teaching assistants, academic leaders, and peer tutors; and she supports new initiatives for faculty and chairs at the four campuses in the University of Missouri System. She earned her PhD in educational psychology from Washington University in St. Louis.

The Course Syllabus

Part I

Focus on Learning

COLLEGES AND UNIVERSITIES across the United States are making a fresh commitment to student learning. Many would argue that learning has always been central in their institutions; however, what is happening now is different in important ways. Barkley, Cross, and Major (2005) remind faculty of the need to pay attention to what students are learning: "At a time when students and parents consider a college education a necessity . . . legislators, accrediting agencies, the American public, and educators themselves are raising questions about what students are learning in college—and they are asking for evidence" (p. xi). These changing expectations about the need for effective undergraduate education are reinforced by broader influences, including the increased use of technology and the short half-life of knowledge in most discipline areas. Lifelong learning—including communication, critical thinking, and team-building skills—is a virtual necessity for all members of the workforce today. Kuh (2007) points out that "as many as four-fifths of high-school graduates will need some form of postsecondary education if they are to become self-sufficient and the nation is to remain economically competitive" (p. B12). The nature of the workforce and the diverse student populations that feed it also call for new innovations in the classroom.

Along with the recognition of multiple perspectives comes a responsibility that colleges and universities are trying to meet through a renewed focus on students and how they learn. As an instructor, making your students' learning and development a priority means that you must consider their varied educational needs, interests, and motivations as you determine the content and structure of your course.

Barr and Tagg's (1995) influential article "From Teaching to Learning: A New Paradigm for Undergraduate Education" fueled a healthy movement toward rethinking the nature of teaching and learning. It was followed by Tagg's (2003) book *The Learning Paradigm College*. The Association of American Colleges and Universities (2002) released an important monograph, *Greater Expectations: A New Vision for Learning as a Nation Goes to*

College, that also sparked campus symposia and discussions. Subsequent books—such as Weimer's (2002) *Learner-Centered Teaching* and Fink's (2003) *Creating Significant Learning Experiences*—and numerous articles provide useful models and convincing research. A number of recent publications have reinforced the need for more attention to instructional processes in part because of the influx of so-called Millennials, students born after 1982 who often enter colleges and universities without adequate academic preparation, study skills, or the predisposition to do whatever it takes to succeed.

Much has been written about the Millennial generation. McGuire and Williams (2002) characterize Millennials as having a consumer mentality, ubiquitous computer access, and an intolerance for nonengaging pedagogical techniques (p. 186). The Millennials are also characterized as being team oriented. Howe, Strauss, and Matson (2000) state, "From Barney and soccer to school uniforms and a new classroom emphasis on group learning, Millennials are developing strong team instincts and tight peer bonds" (p. 44). Carlson (2005), quoting R. T. Sweeney, adds, "'In grade school they were pushed to collaboration' which explains the popularity of group study in college today . . . 'The collaboration . . . is both in-person and virtual'" (p. A36).

Furthermore, Millennials are focused on being credentialed with little interest in obtaining a broad-based liberal arts education. Thus, they are concerned with careers and earning a good living. Bauerlein (2006) regards Millennials as disengaged from the liberal arts curriculum and focused instead on "a blooming, buzzing confusion of adolescent stimuli," such as "TV shows, blogs, hand-helds, [and] wireless" (p. B8). Sweeney remarks on the rigidity of the Millennials: "They want to learn, but they want to learn only what they have to learn, and they want to learn it in a style that is best for them . . . Often they prefer to learn by doing" (Carlson, 2005, p. A36). Strauss and Howe (2005) offer a stern warning that faculty have to change to face these realities: "[I]f Millennials perceive professors as being so stuck in the last century on matters of ideology, attitude, and technology that they can no longer teach the knowledge and skills necessary for financial success—then colleges should watch out. Many will see their admissions pools shrink, their acceptance yields decline, and their dropout rates rise—perhaps sharply" (p. B24).

More positively, Harris and Cullen (2007) note that the Millennials' penchant for "doing rather than knowing" leads them to favor experiential learning and trial and error over abstract knowledge, an observation supporting the shift toward a learning-centered pedagogy (p. 5).

Preparing Students

The Association of College and Research Libraries (2006) defines information-literate students as those who "recognize when information is needed and have the ability to locate, evaluate, and use effectively the needed information." As the world moves toward a knowledge-based economy, information literacy becomes a crucial component of preparing students for the lifelong learning that current and future job markets demand.

You need only consider the situations students will face after graduation to appreciate the importance of a focus on learning for your course and your syllabus. Our contemporary lives have intensified our need to know how to learn, both alone and in collaboration with others. Upon leaving school, your students will encounter complex problems daily and will come to recognize that contradiction, ambiguity, and change are natural states of affairs. Faced with multiple and often conflicting perspectives, they will continually be forced to break out of old thought patterns, to think in new ways. The Association of American Colleges and Universities (2002) frames it this way: "The world is complex, interconnected, and more reliant on knowledge than ever before. College has become a virtual necessity for individuals to build satisfying lives and careers. In a world of turbulent changes, every kind of occupation has seen a dramatic increase in education requirements. The majority of jobs considered desirable are now held by people with at least some college, and jobs for the best educated workers are growing the fastest" (chap. 1).

Preparing your students for the purposeful and effective lifelong learning that these conditions require has strong implications for course content, structure, and the materials and strategies that you use to promote learning. Students will require more carefully thought-out information and well-honed tools.

Our students live and work in a world where the quality and quantity of information changes rapidly and what counts as knowledge alters with time and context. The effects of information technology and communications technology have produced profound changes in the way we live and work. Baron (2001) reminds us that:

> *Information sources have proliferated and become more complex over the past decade, and they will continue to do so for a long time to come. From a well-established, systemic, and centralized system composed mainly of books, journals, government documents, and the indices that accompany them, the world of information has expanded tremendously.*

It now includes not only online versions of all of the traditional sources, but also sources never before considered, such as electronic databases and Web sites. The sheer volume of information and information sources is daunting, and so is the task of making informed and discriminating choices of value and usage.

An impressive number of new studies, books, and articles have focused on the way students learn. Bransford, Brown, and Cocking's (2000) *How People Learn* made it difficult for even the most lecture-committed faculty member to ignore research with clear implications for a more learning-centered basis of teaching. Beichner's (2006) groundbreaking summary of the research on active learning and its implications for all aspects of teaching and learning, including the design of learning environments, makes it difficult to ignore the mounting evidence that business as usual—preparing and delivering lectures to passive students who then regurgitate "the facts" on short-answer or multiple-choice tests—is no longer an adequate pedagogical response to the demands of the twenty-first century. In fact, Finkle (2000) concludes, "Educational research over the past twenty-five years has established beyond a doubt a simple fact: What is transmitted to students through lecturing is simply not retained for any significant length of time" (p. 3).

Setting a Framework for Knowledge

Learning is an active, constructive, contextual process. New knowledge is acquired in relation to previous knowledge; information becomes meaningful when it is presented and acquired in some type of framework. From a learning-centered perspective, your task as an instructor is to interact with students in ways that enable them to acquire new information, practice new skills, reconfigure what they already know, and recognize what they have learned (B. G. Davis, 1993).

A learning-centered approach has subtle but profound implications for you as a teacher. It asks that you think carefully about your teaching philosophy, what it means to be an educated person in your discipline or field, how your course relates to disciplinary and interdisciplinary programs of study, and your intentions and purposes for producing and assessing learning. It asks that you think through the implications of your preferred teaching style; the decisions you make about teaching strategies and forms of assessment; and the ways that students' diverse needs, interests, and purposes can influence all those choices.

Clarifying Expectations

The syllabus provides the first opportunity faculty have to encourage and guide students to take responsibility for their learning. Weimer (2002) argues that teaching students to be responsible, and therefore successful, in their academic pursuits sets learning-centered instruction apart from teacher-centered instruction. When reading a learning-centered syllabus, students learn what is required to achieve the course objectives, *and* they learn what processes will support their academic success. In addition to stating what students will know at the conclusion of the course, objectives may also address the skills students will learn to achieve those competencies. Examples of this are learning the oratory skills necessary to present an oral argument, learning the interpersonal skills needed to work successfully in a small group, and learning to use software effectively to support a presentation on a research project. Technically speaking, these skills are not necessarily content knowledge for law, business, or advanced research methods courses, but within learning-centered courses, they are acknowledged outcomes because they are integrally connected to attaining academic success. In a learning-centered course, both content and process skills may be included as outcomes. If you require students to write persuasive statements comparing materials that they have read, you must take responsibility for ensuring that they know how to do so.

A key expectation may be helping students learn to become what the Association of American Colleges and Universities (2002) defines as "intentional learners":

> *In a turbulent and complex world, every college student will need to be purposeful and self-directed in multiple ways. Purpose implies clear goals, an understanding of process, and appropriate action. Further, purpose implies intention in one's actions. Becoming such an intentional learner means developing self-awareness about the reason for study, the learning process itself, and how education is used. Intentional learners are integrative thinkers who can see connections in seemingly disparate information and draw on a wide range of knowledge to make decisions. They adapt the skills learned in one situation to problems encountered in another: in a classroom, the workplace, their communities, or their personal lives. As a result, intentional learners succeed even when instability is the only constant.*

Sections of the syllabus can communicate not only what *you* will do to help students meet course objectives but also what *students* can do to meet the objectives. Two places in the syllabus where you can convey these responsibilities and reinforce the rationale for the course's design are in sections that explain your teaching philosophy and your expectations and policies.

Teaching Philosophy

Including a teaching philosophy statement in your syllabus sends a strong message that you are thoughtful about your instructional work and that you've considered carefully what contributes to a successful course. Such a statement introduces you to your students and sets a tone for the term. The statement may address your plan for accomplishing course goals and focus on the learning climate you intend to create. In their philosophy statement, many faculty colleagues describe their understanding of the learning process and how their class routines, activities, and assignments are consistent with that understanding. This statement makes very clear what you value about teaching and learning and tells students that you intend to share this process with them.

Teaching philosophy statements are typically two to three pages long and are most often written to accompany application materials for an academic position or for tenure and promotion review. You will want to reduce your initial lengthy statement to a long paragraph of about two hundred to three hundred words that can be included in the syllabus. Chism (1998) and Goodyear and Allchin (1998) offer succinct guides for constructing a teaching philosophy statement. As the frequency of reviewing course syllabi for evaluating teaching increases (Seldin, 1998, 2004, 2007), disciplinary experts are asked to judge syllabi for their scholarship and for promotion and tenure with the goal of evaluating how completely the syllabus demonstrates "both the instructor's mastery of the subject matter and ability to make this subject matter accessible to students" (Albers, 2003, p. 70). A teaching philosophy statement suggests that both of these criteria are valued.

Expectations, Responsibilities, and Policies

Outlining the policies and procedures that undergird the instructional work planned for the term offers another opportunity to convey your expectations, requirements, and standards for coursework and student behaviors. Consider including statements that describe your policies on attendance (including absences, tardiness, and the consequences of either); procedures for submitting written work, lab reports, and homework (including submitting work after its due date); and policies for extra credit, make-up tests, and assigning delayed grades. Addressing each of these expectations completely in the syllabus clarifies the procedures from the start of the quarter or semester, ensures that students have access to this essential information, and, over time, may offer you and your students more instructional time on task.

Creating programmatic policies with departmental colleagues offers another way to increase instructional time and to reduce time spent negotiating and arbitrating procedural issues. When faculty who teach sections of a course or who teach courses in a major or program develop and consistently use guidelines, students progress through the requirements informed about common procedures and policies. Less time, therefore, is spent confronting misbehaviors or violations, and more time is available for learning. Guidelines that are unusual or unique to a particular course or instructor may confuse students accustomed to following and respecting common procedures. Disciplinary societies and associations may provide the rationale for encouraging faculty colleagues in a department to agree on a common set of course expectations. Many professional organizations have codes of conduct and ethics that can be adopted directly or adapted as instructional or programmatic policies of academic honesty. Similarly, the manuscript submission guidelines in place for journals published by disciplinary societies may offer reasonable guidelines—on spacing, fonts, formats for citations and references, and the like—to adopt programmatically for written assignments. When expectations for academic honesty and writing in the discipline are developed and adopted as departmental policy, then faculty colleagues send a common message of their intent to help students develop as professionals in the discipline. Just as you want to help students learn to think like historians or sociologists, you can help them learn the conduct codes and writing conventions used in the discipline. These policies and expectations add an additional avenue for reinforcing the dual focus on content and process.

Statements of civility and disability access are becoming standard sections of the course syllabus on most campuses. Both topics refer to respecting others, and since society is increasingly consumer oriented and litigious, many colleagues, including deans and other academic leaders, think that it's vital to devote attention in the course syllabus to those issues. Each issue may be addressed effectively in institutional policies that ensure that all members of the campus community have equal access to instructional and campus resources. If that is the case on your campus, use the institutional policies that explain why respectful behaviors must characterize the learning environment and what that means in your course (e.g., be prompt, silence cell phones, raise hands to contribute), and then point students to the URL or manual for the conduct code that brings authority to the policy.

On every campus an office is responsible for ensuring that federal policy guidelines are followed so that classroom accommodations are offered to students with disabilities. The syllabus is a good place to remind students of the campus policy, procedures for adhering to it, and what office to consult if they require accommodations. These procedures generally assign responsibility to the campus office, not the course instructor, to arrange for instructional accommodations for students with disabilities. If you are in the position of creating your own syllabus statements about these two topics, know that guidance for faculty is often available from campus offices and Web sites. If your campus resources are not complete, access the resources for a campus in your Carnegie classification comparator group (McCormick & Zhao, 2005) online at http://www. carnegiefoundation.org/classifications. Colleagues at campuses similar to yours are likely to have accomplished these tasks and made them available publicly so that you can adapt the statements to your course and your campus. When these expectations and guidelines are added to the syllabus and attention is called to them as the course begins and as soon as infractions are apparent, two outcomes are likely: faculty will prevent problems from occurring later in the term, and students will receive consistent messages that they, too, are responsible for creating a classroom climate that fosters learning.

Encouraging Responsibility for Learning

A learning-centered approach asks to what extent you can support and challenge students to assume responsibility for actively shaping their learning in your course and in future courses with the understanding that they will be learning independently throughout life. As you prepare a syllabus that promotes student learning, consider the balance between instructor leadership, student development, and student initiative. Taking into account the level of the course (general education, upper division, graduate, etc.) *and* what we know about students' prerequisite skills and knowledge, you will want to ask yourself for each course activity the extent to which students will be involved in:

- Clarifying their own goals for the course
- Planning tasks that will meet their individual learning goals
- Monitoring and assessing their own progress
- Establishing criteria for judging their own performance

Answers to these queries require respect for the course's educational intentions (including any limitations imposed by certification or licensing), time constraints, and other students' needs. A reasonable strategy is to design learning activities that steer students to accept more responsibility for learning during the course of the current term. Your challenges derive from understanding and meeting the requirements of a diverse group of students who bring to your classroom a broad array of learning, work, family, and life experiences and an equally broad array of expectations.

Acknowledging the Context for Learning

Today's fast-paced high-tech society influences the expectations that Millennials bring to our classrooms (Oblinger, 2003) and bears some responsibility for their consumer attitudes (Groccia, 1997). When our institutions respond to consumer expectations by creating student centers where, in one location, students can buy a meal, arrange financial aid, take placement tests, register for courses, purchase texts, and find personal tutors and other supports for learning, we inadvertently shape students' attitudes to regard the learning experience in the same way as they regard the experience of one-stop shopping. Our faculty colleagues share the concern that such attitudes of entitlement are incompatible with learning. Earning credits presents a different incentive for taking a course than does the intent to learn. Students motivated to learn and master course objectives are different classroom citizens from students motivated solely for grades or credits. A classroom focus on learning presupposes that students have jettisoned their consumer mentality. Making this distinction clear in courses—beginning with messages in your syllabus about your teaching philosophy and expectations, including civility—can help students change their preconceived attitudes or at least be aware that they hold views that are incompatible with a learning-centered classroom.

Engaging students in purposeful and meaningful learning experiences is an obvious strategy for focusing students on learning, but what exactly is engagement? The National Survey of Student Engagement (which is abbreviated NSSE and pronounced "Nessie") was designed to assess the quality of the undergraduate educational experience by surveying first-year and senior students in the spring term (Kuh, 2003). Students describe their learning experiences in class and in cocurricular activities on and off campus by responding to questions that are based on the "Seven Principles for Good Practice in Undergraduate Education" (Chickering & Gamson, 1987). NSSE was piloted in 1999 at seventy-five campuses. Eleven hundred campuses participated in the survey in 2007, so it is reasonable to inquire whether your campus is participating and, if so, how you can obtain the data. This data will offer you an understanding of how students experience learning on your campus. (If your campus does not participate in the survey, an abundance of material about NSSE and the instructional and institutional practices that promote student engagement is available on the Web at http://nsse.iub.edu.)

The NSSE response items represent an array of instructional and campuswide practices derived from the literature on student development and learning; reviewing those items is helpful. Response items are grouped into benchmarks that describe instructional options that challenge students academically, that enrich the instructional experience by creating deep learning experiences, that exemplify active and collaborative learning, that create opportunities for student and faculty interactions in and out of class, and that are available in a supportive campus environment. How campuses are promoting engaging practices and addressing their benchmark data was explored by Kuh, Kinzie, Schuh, Whitt, and Associates (2005) who visited a broad array of campuses with high NSSE scores to learn what practices were in place to support student success and engagement. Recently, a new learning tool has been developed by the same people who created NSSE. Called CLASSE (short for "Classroom Survey of Student Engagement"), it addresses the issue of faculty denial about the broad-based NSSE data: "Oh, that's very interesting, but those aren't *my* students! My students are engaged!" (Rhem, 2007). CLASSE proposes to answer three research questions: "Can we measure levels of student engagement in the classroom? Will levels of student engagement vary as [a] function of how important the instructor views the engagement practice in class? Could these measures of classroom engagement be used to prompt instructional improvement practices?" This two-part instrument (1) surveys faculty to determine the value—based on a four-point Likert scale—they place on specific engagement activities, cognitive skills, other educational practices, and class atmosphere, with an option to add eight course-specific questions, and (2) surveys students about how frequently designated practices occurred in the target class (Ouimet, 2007; Smallwood, 2007).

The implications of this faculty survey for syllabus construction are enormous. Responding to the CLASSE survey guides you to think about your course at the deepest level. Such reflection will help you make choices about where to place your emphasis as you design your course and prepare your syllabus. The CLASSE survey may be more powerful for course decision-making purposes than the long-standing Teaching Goals Inventory (Angelo & Cross, 1993), which is conveniently available online as a self-scoring 53-point survey at several locations, including: http://fm.iowa. uiowa.edu/fmi/xsl/tgi/data_entry.xsl?-db=tgi_data&-lay=Layout01&- view; http://www.siue.edu/~deder/assess/cats/tchgoals.html; http:// campus.umr.edu/assess/tgi/tgi.html; and, http://www.wcer.wisc.edu/ archive/cl1/CL/doingcl/tgi.htm.

Developing a Learning-Centered Syllabus

Adopting a learning-centered approach to courses in higher education is a commitment to considering how each aspect of your course will most effectively support student learning. The commitment brings with it the responsibility to help students learn both content and process. *Process* refers to the skills students will need to meet success as they are learning the content. The reality for many of us is that our students are not as well prepared as we want them to be when they enroll in our courses. Some of our colleagues bitterly attribute this to their K–12 or community college education. In a learning-centered classroom, we are responsible for offering tools and strategies as metacognitive supports that will help our students succeed. On this topic, Fayetteville State University admonishes colleagues to "teach the students you have, not the students you wish you had" (Kuh et al., 2005, p. 78). Accepting that challenge, how, then, can you use your syllabus to promote your students' engagement with subject matter and their intellectual development?

Your syllabus is an important point of interaction between you and your students in and out of class, face-to-face, and online. The traditional syllabus is primarily a source of information, something distributed and, too often, filed after the first day of class. While the learning-centered syllabus does include basic information, it can be an important learning tool to help you:

- Convey to your students what matters to you about learning

- Set a tone for learning and how to learn that students will accept

- Send a message about what students can expect from you and the campus community to support their learning during the term

These goals reflect how Bain (2004) describes the three parts of a "promising syllabus":

Trust, rejection of power, and setting standards that represented authentic goals rather than schoolwork are apparent in the . . . [promising] syllabus the best teachers tended to use . . . First, the instructor would lay out the promises or opportunities that the course offered to students . . . Second, the teacher would explain what the students would be doing to realize those promises, . . . Third, the syllabus summarized how the instructor and the students would understand the nature and the progress of the learning. (pp. 74–75)

Likewise, the learning-centered syllabus reinforces the intentions, roles, attitudes, and strategies that you will use to promote active, purposeful, and effective learning. The sections in the first part of this book will help you plan, compose, and use a learning-centered syllabus. The second part provides excerpts from syllabi in use on campuses across the nation.

The research on learning has enormous implications for faculty. Two areas are of particular interest: the international research on deep versus surface learning and the convergent research presented by Bransford, Brown, and Cocking (2000). The research on deep/surface learning began in the 1970s in Sweden, Great Britain, and Australia (Marton, Hounsell, & Entwistle, 1997). Basically, it suggests that students take either an in-depth or a surface approach to learning and that their approach can be affected by a teacher's assignments and expectations. Four key components—totally consistent with cooperative learning (Millis & Cottell, 1998) practices—characterize a deep, rather than a surface, approach to learning. Rhem (1995) summarizes them as follows:

> *Motivational context: We learn best what we feel a need to know. Intrinsic motivation remains inextricably bound to some level of choice and control. Courses that remove these take away the sense of ownership and kill one of the strongest elements in lasting learning.*
>
> *Learner activity: Deep learning and "doing" travel together. Doing in itself isn't enough. Faculty must connect activity to the abstract conceptions that make sense of it, but passive mental postures lead to superficial learning.*
>
> *Interaction with others: As Noel Entwistle put it in a recent e-mail message, "The teacher is not the only source of instruction or inspiration." Peers working as groups enjoin dimensions of learning that lectures and readings by themselves cannot touch.*
>
> *A well-structured knowledge base: This doesn't just mean presenting new material in an organized way. It also means engaging and reshaping the concepts students bring with them when they register. Deep approaches and learning for understanding are integrative processes. The more fully new concepts can be connected with students' prior experience and existing knowledge, the more it is they will be impatient with inert facts and eager to achieve their own synthesis. (p. 4)*

Deep learning and cooperative group work mesh perfectly when teachers capitalize on the underlying theories by—among other things—developing homework assignments that motivate students to get involved with the knowledge base. Students often become motivated when the material is relevant to their own lives and learning. When students can place content knowledge in a personal context, they are more likely to retain and retrieve the information (the "self-referral" effect). This research is the basis for Jensen's (2000) advice that teachers help students "discover their own connections rather than imposing [their] own" and encouraging "learners to use their own words with regard to new learning" (p. 282).

Bransford, Brown, and Cocking (2000) discuss three fundamental learning principles, which are amply illustrated and applied in a later work, *How Students Learn: History, Mathematics, and Science in the Classroom* (Donovan & Bransford, 2005). The first two principles are fairly well known and accepted by teachers in higher education: (1) Because we must build on what students already bring to our courses, discovering what they know and don't know, including uncovering preconceptions and misconceptions, is critically important. (The work of Angelo and Cross [1993] on classroom assessment techniques dovetails nicely with this learning principle.) (2) Students need deep foundational knowledge that rests on conceptual frameworks that facilitate retrieval and application. For most faculty, deep knowledge is a given. Less understood is the third principle, metacognition—that is, thinking about thinking: (3) Students must know where they are headed and monitor their progress toward learning objectives.

Consider each of these aspects of learning-centered instruction as you plan and develop your syllabus. How you present the structure and rationale for the course syllabus on the first day of the term determines to a large extent how students will focus and what they will learn. It is a document critically important to an engaging course.

Planning Your Learning-Centered Syllabus: An Overview of the Process

As indicated above, composing a learning-centered syllabus is an important stage in the process of crafting educational experiences for your students. The process first requires a well-developed rationale concerning your personal beliefs and assumptions about the nature of learning and how it is promoted and produced. The process requires next that you establish what skills, knowledge, and attitudes you believe are of most worth, how they can be built into your course, and how they will be appropriately assessed.

It requires that you create a learning environment for your students using teaching and learning strategies that are consistent with those beliefs. And finally, it requires that you compose a syllabus that will communicate your expectations and intentions to your students.

Course development is beyond the scope of this guide, but this section will provide an overview of the process that leads to creating your syllabus. The next sections, "Composing a Learning-Centered Syllabus" and "Using a Learning-Centered Syllabus," offer suggestions for ways to communicate these important concepts to your students. Part II provides examples developed and used by faculty in course syllabi and course manuals that adopt a learning-centered perspective. Suggested readings are provided in Part III to help with many of the issues raised here.

Wiggins and McTighe (2005) urge faculty to design courses by beginning with the end in mind and looking at three stages:

Stage 1: What is worthy and requiring of understanding? (In other words, let your course focus on what the authors characterize as "essential understandings"—what students must take away from your course. You want to "go deep" in those areas.

Stage 2: What is evidence of understanding? (These are your assessment/evaluation practices, both formal and informal.)

Stage 3: What learning experiences and teaching promote understanding, interest and excellence? (These are the active engagements in learning that help students master your material.)

Fink's (2003) "backwards design" model builds on this concept by suggesting a taxonomy consistent with it that adds dimensions of learning, including these elements: foundational knowledge, application, integration, human dimensions, caring, and learning how to learn. This taxonomy goes beyond Bloom's (1956) familiar focus on content knowledge by including additional features that faculty identify when they envision students who have completed the course. These goals often involve intangibles that are difficult to measure, but immensely important, such as "valuing" or "appreciating." Thus, in planning your syllabus, first identify your learning goals and outcomes. Then consider the assessment approaches—both informal and formal—that will help you know whether your students are actually learning what you proposed as outcomes. The final piece is determining what assignments and activities will promote these learning outcomes.

Nilson (2002, 2003) offers another dimension of planning the syllabus. She suggests creating a graphic syllabus to supplement your learning-centered one. This could be a one-page diagram, a flowchart, or a concept map of the topical organization of the course. To complement the graphic syllabus, she suggests distributing an outcomes map that displays the course outcomes. Students who favor a visual learning style will be especially appreciative of the perspective offered by these graphic supports.

Develop a Well-Grounded Rationale for Your Course

The composition of your syllabus is integrally tied to your rationale for the design of the course. All aspects of your course are influenced by the sometimes-taken-for-granted beliefs and implicit assumptions that frame how you think about and practice the educational process. A well-grounded rationale for your practice is, according to Shulman (2004), "a set of critically examined core assumptions about why you do what you do in the way that you do it" and will help you make decisions about what to include in your syllabus. Shulman also suggests that reflecting on your teaching is an act of scholarship. The questions he suggests to guide reflection are summarized in "Scholarly Reflection about Teaching."

Wlodkowski and Ginsberg (1995) suggest that as you develop your syllabus, you should check it for bias. Scan the entire syllabus for the norms it reflects, and think about how you might remodel your course and your syllabus to be more intellectually and culturally responsive. Changes you make in your syllabus can profoundly affect the learning process and clarify your expectations of how the knowledge of the course is constructed.

Scholarly Reflection about Teaching

Shulman (2004) suggests that you think about the ways your course and syllabus represent acts of scholarship. Adopt a stance of inquiry toward your practice, seeing your ideas and practices in constant formation and always in need of further investigation. Before composing the syllabus, engage in scholarly reflection about your teaching.

In particular, Shulman suggests that you consider the following:

- Every course we craft is a lens into our fields and our personal conceptions of those disciplines. Give careful thought to the shape and content of your course as if it were a *scholarly argument*.

What is the thesis of the argument and its main points? What are the key bodies of evidence? How does the course begin? Why does it begin where it does? How does it end? Why does it end as it does? Most scholarly arguments carry the intention to persuade. What do you want to persuade your students to believe? Or question? Or do you want them to develop new appetites or dispositions?

- How can a colleague develop a sense of you as a scholar by examining the various features of your course? In your field, or even in your own department, are there distinctly different ways

(Continued)

to organize your course—ways that reflect quite different perspectives on your discipline or field? Do you focus on particular topics while your colleagues might make other choices? Why?

• In what ways does your course teach students how scholars work in your field? How does it teach the methods, procedures, and values that shape how knowledge claims are made and adjudicated within your field? How does it open doors to the critical dialogues and key arguments that scholars are engaged in at the cutting edge of your field?

• How does your course connect with other courses in your own or other fields? To what extent does your course provide a foundation for others that follow it? Or build on what students have already (one silently prays) learned in other courses? Or challenge and contradict what students are learning in your own or other disciplines? How, in general, does your course fit within a larger conception of curriculum, program, or undergraduate experience?

• What do you expect students to find particularly fascinating about your course? Where will they encounter the greatest difficulties of either understanding or motivation? How does the content of your course connect to matters that your students already understand or have experienced? Where will it seem most alien? How do you address these common student responses in your course? How has the course evolved over time in response to them?

• Lastly, you might try playing with some metaphors for characterizing your course and its place in the larger curriculum or in the broader intellectual and moral lives of your students. Is your course like a journey, a parable, a football game, a museum, a romance, a concerto, an Aristotelian tragedy, an obstacle course, one or all of the above? How can your metaphor(s) illuminate key aspects of your course?

Decide on Desired Outcomes and Assessment Measures

Plan your course with process, content, and product goals in mind. For example, in addition to the conceptual knowledge and technical skills of a discipline or field, your students will need other tools for living and working effectively in society. Students should be able to do the following:

• Initiate, understand, assess, and assume responsibility for their own ongoing learning processes

• Access and use resources effectively

• Work alone and collaborate with others

• Resolve dilemmas that emerge from complex situations

• Think and communicate effectively using appropriate means, such as writing, speaking and listening, numbers, graphics, electronic technologies, 3D forms, or performance

• Clarify personal values, purposes, and goals

• Understand and respect differences

Whenever you formulate learning goals, you should simultaneously address assessment procedures. Huba and Freed (2000) remind us that assessment is a central part of learner-centered teaching. "When we assess our students' learning, we force the questions, 'What have our students learned and how well have they learned it? How successful have we been at what we are trying to accomplish?' Because of this focus on learning, assessment in higher education is sometimes referred to as outcomes assessment or student outcomes assessment" (p. 8). Become more conscious of your assessment philosophy and develop an understanding of how your approach to assessment fits with your beliefs about teaching and learning. Use multiple measures to avoid limiting judgments to one or two high-stakes testing occasions or one particular kind of assessment task. Wlodkowski and Ginsberg (1995) recommend the following norms for developing an assessment philosophy:

- The assessment process is connected to the learners' world, frames of reference, and values.

- Demonstration of learning includes multiple ways to represent knowledge and skills and allows students to attain outcomes at different points in time.

- Self-assessment is essential to the overall assessment process.

As your students accept increasing responsibility for their learning, they must develop the tools for self-assessment that will help them improve on and internalize criteria for monitoring and judging their own performance. You can establish creative forms of evaluation beyond paper-and-pencil tests, with clearly stated standards and criteria, that will provide useful and ongoing information for both you and your students (J. R. Davis, 1993). Examples of such creative evaluations include product assessment (essays, stories, research reports, writing portfolios, projects, etc.); performance assessments (music, dance, dramatic performance, science lab demonstrations, debates, experiments, action research, etc.); and process-focused assessment (oral questioning, interviews, learning logs, process folios, journals, observation, etc.) (Wlodkowski & Ginsberg, 1995). It is important that your assessment and grading strategies are consistent with your rationale.

If your evaluation criteria are clearly understood and seem fair to your students, then they can more easily evaluate their own work and be more assured about the results. When students participate in determining the criteria by which work will be judged and then play a role in assessing their work (or the work of other students) against those criteria, their personal sense of responsibility for learning is more apparent. This is an important learning experience in itself.

Define and Delimit Course Content

Be clear about what is most worth knowing. Wiggins and McTighe (2004) urge faculty to look at content in terms of the final learning outcomes and to emphasize "enduring understanding," the crucial knowledge that students must take away and retain from a course. The use of active learning may limit the amount of content you can cover in a course, but much of the conceptual material many instructors now cover is poorly learned and soon forgotten. Choose the outcomes you value most. Discipline yourself to prune away forgettable content, and focus on the more important knowledge, skills, and values (B. G. Davis, 1993).

Another way of thinking about content is to place it in three categories: content that all students will be required to know, content that you will make available to support individual student inquiry or projects, and content that might be of interest only to a student who wants to specialize in this area. Excessive emphasis on transmission of large quantities of information infringes on the time students need to transform that information into useful knowledge (Kurfiss, 1988). Develop a conceptual framework (a theory, theme, or controversial issue) that will support major ideas and topics. If critical thinking is one of your goals for students, what questions, issues, and problems can frame your course? A summary of principles that foster critical thinking is provided in "Principles for Designing a Course That Fosters Critical Thinking."

Structure Your Students' Active Involvement in Learning

Decide what topics are appropriate to what types of student activities and assignments. Will your course topics tend toward a content or a process orientation? Which activities and types of products can involve students in sustained intensive work, both independently and with one another? What activities will help students learn the tools of the discipline or field? How can you develop a challenging and supportive course climate that builds student effectiveness, teaches interpersonal and collaborative skills, and develops the capacity for lifelong learning? What strategies will you use to shape basic skills and procedures, present information, guide inquiry, monitor individual and group activities, and support and challenge critical reflection?

J. R. Davis (1993) advocates an eclectic approach, using the strengths of teaching and learning strategies to achieve different purposes. General instructional strategies include training and coaching, lecturing and explaining, inquiry and discovery, groups and teams, and experience and reflection. Davis emphasizes that to be effective, the strategies you choose must fit with the outcomes you hope to achieve. Implementing a strategy involves making the strategy work for the subject; the setting; and the varied capacities, knowledge, skills, and experiences of these students.

Principles for Designing a Course That Fosters Critical Thinking

Just as Miss America contestants routinely told Bert Parks they wished for world peace, many faculty members, when asked about hopes for their courses, respond, "I want my students to learn to think critically." Streck (2007) verifies this conclusion through answers collected from a key question: "If you only had your students for a week, what would you want them to learn?" Critical thinking skills are always listed. However, all faculty recognize that fundamental knowledge (content) is critical if students are to advance to higher levels of learning. Thus, a key question becomes, how do we—experts in our disciplines—"balance content with some aspects of critical thinking" (p. 9)? Bean (1996) argues the premise "that integrating writing and other critical thinking activities into a course increases students' learning while teaching them thinking skills for posing questions, proposing hypotheses, gathering and analyzing data, and making arguments" (p. 1).

Bean urges faculty to plan courses—and thus to develop syllabi that reflect that plan—by focusing from the start on critical thinking objectives. He directs them to the work of Kurfiss (1988). From her examination of a wide number of courses, Kurfiss derived eight principles for designing courses that support critical thinking, recognizing elements common to all disciplines.

1. Critical thinking is a learnable skill; the instructor and peers are resources in developing critical thinking skills.

2. Problems, questions, or issues are the point of entry into the subject and a source of motivation for sustained inquiry.

3. Successful courses balance the challenges to think critically with support tailored to students' developmental needs.

4. Courses are assignment centered rather than text and lecture centered. Goals, methods, and evaluation emphasize using content rather than simply acquiring it.

5. Students are required to formulate their ideas in writing or other appropriate modes.

6. Students collaborate to learn and to stretch their thinking, for example, in pair problem solving and small-group work.

7. Several courses, particularly those that teach problem-solving skills, nurture students' metacognitive abilities.

8. The developmental needs of students are acknowledged and used as information in the design of the course. Teachers in these courses make standards explicit and then help students learn how to achieve them. (pp. 88–89)

Identify and Assemble Resources Required for Active Learning

Active thinkers—those engaged in speaking and listening, reading, writing, and reflecting about a topic of interest—assemble a rich array of resources (people, materials, and strategies) to facilitate their creative intellectual activity, both alone and in collaboration with others. You can specify a core or central body of information and "seed the environment" with other ideas and concepts that you value (Brown et al., 1993). Consider ways to include alternate and conflicting perspectives through lectures, debates, panel presentations, demonstrations, books, and readings. Also consider films, CDs, DVDs, maps, libraries, museums, theaters, studios, labs, databases, Internet sites, and other materials that students can appropriate and transform through personal interpretation and new technologies. Many publishers augment their textbooks with supplementary materials and instructor manuals. Consult the resources available for the courses you teach because many of these supplements can be adapted for exercises, activities, and small-group discussions in class or online.

You can challenge students to search for further information or new, even contradictory, points of view that may be relevant to the issues, questions, and problems that the class is investigating. Your guidance will be especially helpful as they learn to sift through a morass of Web-based information and determine what is valid and what is problematic.

Request Permission to Use Copyrighted Material

When assembling your course readings and other course materials, be sure to obtain the necessary permission from the copyright owner before duplicating articles, graphics, or other materials that you want to include. Fair use does not allow for extensive or repeated copying. Securing copyright permissions can be a time-consuming and costly process.

Authors are protected by federal statute against unauthorized use of their unpublished manuscripts. Under the Copyright Act of 1976 (Title 17 of the *United States Code*), an unpublished work is copyrighted from the moment it is fixed in tangible form—for example, typed on a page. Copyright protection is "an incident of the process of authorship" (U.S. Copyright Office, 1981). Until the author formally transfers copyright, the author owns the copyright on an unpublished manuscript, and all exclusive rights due the owner of a copyright of a published work are also due the author of an unpublished work. To ensure copyright protection, include the copyright notice on all published works. The notice need not appear on unpublished materials. Registration of copyright provides a public record and is usually a prerequisite for legal action.

To request permission to reprint, you must first contact the copyright holder. When the holder is a publishing house, contact its copyright department to find out what is required. Some publishers use a copyright clearing house. Typically, you will need to provide the author, book title, ISBN, publisher, chapter/article title, number of copies, number of pages, college/university, course title, and instructor, as well as a copy of what you are requesting permission to use. You can mail or fax a letter to the publisher or the clearing house to provide this information. Getting permission to reprint typically takes six to eight weeks, so plan to begin the process at least two months before your syllabus will be distributed with required resources. Online clearing houses, such as the Copyright Clearance Center (http://www.copyright.com), will accept an online request and, for a fee, seek the permissions on your behalf.

Move from Planning to Composing

Once your rationale and outcomes are clear and you know (1) your course's significant content and process goals; (2) the opportunities you will provide for active, productive thinking about significant questions, issues, and problems in your field; and (3) which avenues you'll take to assess learning, one critical question remains: how will you introduce these ideas to your students? The next section discusses some possible functions for your syllabus.

Composing a Learning-Centered Syllabus

In higher education, every course, every group of students, every instructor, and every individual student is unique, and their particular combination of features will influence the content and form of a syllabus. Your syllabus can be a brief document or an extended text affording a view of your course and its significance. Regardless of your focus—traditional or learning centered—it is essential to include some basic information.

Syllabus Content

Students generally have key questions about a course: Who is teaching it? What is the purpose? What prerequisites, preparation, or skills are expected? What will occur during typical class sessions? What are the required textbooks, course packs, or supplies, such as calculators, art supplies, or personal response systems (more commonly known as "clickers")? What topics will be covered? Will the course be entirely face-to-face, online, or a hybrid? How many and what types of tests will the class take? What types of assignments are required? When are they due? What is the grading system? What are the policies for attendance, late work, and make-up work? It is important to include campus polices on academic honesty, access to services for the disabled, and statements about student conduct and behavior on campus and in class. If you are preparing a syllabus for the first time, beginning with these features is a good starting point.

A learning-centered approach to composing a syllabus incorporates these features but goes further, focusing on the value of your syllabus as a learning tool in your course. It can convey the logic and organization of the course and clarify instructional priorities, providing a common plan and reference. Your syllabus can clarify the responsibilities that both you and your students will assume to achieve the course goals. It can provide students with a way to assess your whole course plan and its rationale, content, activities, policies, and scheduling to achieve some personal control and ownership over their learning processes (Svinicki, 2004; Tagg, 2003). The more we tell students about what to expect in a course by addressing these details and removing from the syllabus and the course the unknowns and the guessing games, the likelier we are to enlist students' interest and cooperation. The syllabus becomes an invitation to share responsibility for successful learning.

A learning-centered syllabus includes more, rather than less, information. It provides students with the resources of a course manual, with each component crafted to promote their learning. Fortunately, if your department is concerned about the costs of copying lengthy documents, you can probably upload these documents and make them available to students on a Web page or at a course management site, such as WebCampus or Blackboard. On the first day of class when you usually distribute and discuss the syllabus, it is best to distribute hard copies even when the syllabus is available electronically. Too few students may have taken the initiative to download it, print it, and bring it to class. But afterwards, students can be responsible for printing additional copies rather than expecting you to provide them.

Syllabus Form

When you lay out your syllabus, remember that it is a reference document that is often read section by section. Instructors handle this in different ways: with emphatic headings, mechanical breaks, or other spatial arrangements that clearly demarcate material and make the readings, grading policy, schedule, and so forth easy for students to read and locate. Some instructors include icons, clip art, or photos to add interest and serve as easy reference points. Increasingly, campus centers for teaching and learning provide formats and templates for developing a syllabus. At some campuses, academic leaders, including deans and chairs, are weighing in on what belongs in a syllabus. As you consider the format you'll use, check the resources on your campus to see whether there is a preferred or recommended format.

It is helpful to distribute longer versions of a syllabus printed on three-hole-punched pages that can be inserted in a three-ring binder. Students appreciate this format because they can then include their own notes and personal resources for the course in one location.

Syllabus Online

Uploading the syllabus to a course management site or to a department's home page offers faculty the opportunity to take advantage of the hypertext environment, to make additions readily available, to announce modifications in scheduled dates, and to create links to other resources for students. Most of us still want and require students to have a hard copy for common reference in the classroom. It is helpful to regard the syllabus as both a dynamic learning tool and an agreement that is reviewed carefully during the first class meetings and returned to frequently throughout the course.

Before placing course material online or in a course management system, you may want to consult with an instructional designer to discuss how to take advantage of the campus computing environment without compromising your goals for students' learning (Smith & Stalcup, 2001; Wilhite, Lunde, & King, 2001). Know how students will be accessing your course materials: from on-campus computer networks—such as labs, classrooms, and residence halls—or from an off-site location such as home or the local library. This is important because it affects connection speed. Faster connection speeds allow for the use of video and audio clips, streaming video, and high-resolution visual images. Slower services, such as dial-up, will be problematic and disadvantage students who do not have access to high-speed service.

Learn which browser, word processor, and other basic software is recommended for the specific course management system you are using. Include that information in the syllabus. For example, if WordPerfect is not compatible (i.e., not readable) with one or more of the systems, directing students to save their files in rich text format (RTF) or portable document format (PDF) will be the workable solution. Keep in mind that your course materials must be in compliance with federal regulations that focus on accessibility.

All Web documents are created using hypertext mark-up language (HTML), the basic programming language of the Web. Many new software products have been developed that make creating HTML documents almost as easy as using standard word-processing software. Microsoft and

WordPerfect have HTML add-ons to their word processors. Those wishing to explore more sophisticated high-end technology can use Java, JavaScript, Flash, and CGI to add interactivity or animation.

Once you've created your Web pages, you will need to work with your college or university computing staff to move your Web pages to the institution's server (unless you or your department runs a server). If you wish to give access only to students in your class, request that your Web server administrator create usernames and passwords for each student.

The first week of the course may be a good time to demonstrate how to access the online course materials. It is also a good time to involve students' class participation by soliciting their recommendations and experiences with Internet service providers and learning which students are willing to be peer mentors for those new to the course management system. Point your students to information technology supports on campus so that they can learn which campus labs have the software necessary to review course materials, and explain how to access campus servers from off campus. Describe how technology will be used in the course to enhance learning objectives. Identify computer hardware and software requirements (such as a Web browser or the course management system choices on your campus) for your students.

Given today's very diverse student body, students' technological competencies and abilities will vary (Oblinger & Oblinger, 2006). Students with visual impairments may not be able to view Web pages unless they have the option to modify text sizes. Optical scanners cannot read some Web pages well. Students may welcome the option to review a lecture by listening to a podcast or to create a podcast in lieu of a written response to an assignment. Students with hearing impairments may not have access to audio files. Work with the campus offices for disability services in advance to ensure that all course materials, online or in class, can be adapted, if necessary, for students in your courses.

Anticipate the inevitable technical questions that all students will have and the problems that they will need to resolve, and be prepared to refer all students to the technical supports and computing labs available to them when they are on campus and when they are accessing campus technology from a distance.

Instructors who put course syllabi online can link them to resources around the world. The syllabus can be easily updated as new resources become available and can provide students with a current picture of course requirements. Homework assignments can be directly linked online to the class schedule and to the grade book. Managing course content, increasing opportunities for interactions between and with your students, and linking students to multiple worldwide resources are the tangible benefits of integrating technology into your course. Oblinger and Hawkins (2005) note that the benefits of technology will soon be ubiquitous in higher education and suggest that technology is moving to the background and "taking its proper place as an enabler rather than as a focus" of the learning process (p. 15).

Syllabus Functions

Your syllabus can serve a wide variety of functions that will support, engage, and challenge students as they participate in instructional activities.

Establishes an Early Point of Contact and Connection between Student and Instructor

The research on NSSE and student engagement (Kuh et al., 2005) clearly shows that students want more frequent interaction with faculty. You can begin to communicate your availability by including basic information, such as your name, address, telephone number, e-mail address, and office and learning lab hours, including instructions on how to arrange for a conference. You can include similar information about other important student contacts—such as TAs, technicians, staff in the department office, and librarians—when appropriate. This contact information will be useful in case plans change during the course of the term or semester. Consider including an information page that solicits students' biographical information (including their address, phone number, e-mail address, etc.) that will help you learn their names, their interests, and why they are in the course. This may also be a vehicle for checking that students completed required prerequisite courses. Consider adding some questions that will give you insights into students' learning styles and their prior educational background. Ask them, for example, why they came to your university. (You can learn a lot about student motivation when you read answers such as, "My parents made me come here," "I am excited about the Ecology program," or "This is the only place that would accept me.") Ask them what they want to learn from your course (this question can often uncover misconceptions and "disconnects"). Ask them to tell you what another instructor did that aided their learning (this question will give you insights into their learning style and also give you a chance to contact a campus colleague to talk about teaching).

To encourage interactions with other students in the course, give students an opportunity to exchange contact information with one another. If you are using a course management system such as Blackboard or Webcampus, show students how to use the system to send messages to everyone or to individual classmates and emphasize that these interactions are a valuable part of learning. Threaded discussions and interactive online activities on these networks are an invaluable way to foster discussions beyond the classroom in hybrid classes and in online courses.

Although campus directories may be public and available to everyone in your campus community, the Family Educational Rights and Privacy Act prohibits directory information (names, addresses, telephone numbers, e-mail addresses, etc.) from being released without allowing students to opt out of the directory. Since you will not know which students have made this request, the student-friendly practice of distributing course rosters is not only outdated but may lead to legal sanctions. Instead, encourage students to get to know each other in class and exchange contact information, and suggest that they begin relying on the course management system's discussion options to form study groups and to make arrangements to do group assignments out of class.

Helps Set the Tone for Your Course

Your syllabus communicates your attitudes toward students and learning. The way in which you communicate your views helps students understand whether your class will be conducted in a formal or informal manner. Communicating an openness to questions, concerns, and dialogue begins with the syllabus and reduces the mystery that inhibits many students' learning. Sending a message to students that you respect the knowledge they bring to the learning setting is another way to set the tone for the course. Consider starting a "questions about the course" thread in an online discussion section of the course management system. Encourage students to respond to each other's questions about an assignment or activity, and explain that you'll chime in if you notice any misleading responses. This sets a tone that student-to-student interactions are valued just as faculty-to-student interactions are.

Describes Your Beliefs about Educational Purposes

You can explain why your course includes objectives that are both content and process oriented and how those objectives determine your expectations of students. Explain how you have set your agenda for the course, how the course structure reinforces goals and objectives, and how the activities and assignments will help students meet both content and process goals. You may describe the learning strategies and techniques that you will use and your rationale for using them. You can make explicit how your criteria and standards for students' work processes and products are aligned with course goals, general education requirements, and/or program goals and outcomes. Refer students to your teaching philosophy statement as evidence of how these practices are consistent with your beliefs.

Acquaints Students with the Logistics of the Course

Courses vary in terms of the days classes meet, the instructors for each class, and the type of sessions that occur (guest lecturers, lab or clinical settings, teamwork sessions, simulations, DVDs, etc.). Your syllabus can detail this information so that students will know what to expect and can be prepared for each class meeting. Providing students with a course calendar helps them plan their work. Request that students notify you as soon as possible about religious observances and business or athletic travel that will affect their class attendance. Noting holidays and any days on which class will be canceled or rescheduled allows students to plan ahead and prevents misunderstandings. Conveying attention to these logistic details shows your sensitivity to diversity and your respect for the value of students' time. Consider including significant dates from the registrar's office on the calendar so that it is very clear, for example, when the last registration and drop dates are for the term. This will increase not only the likelihood that students are aware of these dates but also reinforce the idea that it is their responsibility to adhere to these dates.

Contains Collected Handouts

Faculty often distribute handouts throughout the semester as those documents relate to the topics covered. When students simply stuff them into whatever notebook or file folder is at hand, they often have difficulty retrieving them. Preparing in advance the necessary handouts and including them in the syllabus helps students keep all course material accessible. These items might include student information forms, detailed information on assignments, and various evaluation forms (including rubrics, diagrams, in-class exercises, and other visual representations). An alternative way to distribute a great deal of course material is to work with the campus printing office to duplicate and bind the handouts into a course packet that the bookstore can sell with course textbooks. Course management systems, such as Blackboard or WebCampus, include a variety of folders where course documents, handouts, and assignments can be stored online and downloaded at designated times during the term for reviewing and/or printing.

Defines Student Responsibilities for Successful Coursework

Your syllabus can help students achieve some personal control over their learning, plan their semester, and manage their time effectively. If your students have a clear idea of *what* they are expected to accomplish, *when* they are expected to accomplish it, and even *why* they are asked to do a particular assignment, they will be more likely to finish those assignments within a reasonable time and be appropriately prepared for classes and exams. When the course syllabus outlines campus and instructor policies for academically honest work, respectful and civil classroom behaviors, and effective interpersonal and group behaviors, students learn to value and adopt professional behaviors so that they know *how* to interact throughout their careers and adulthood.

Describes Active Learning

Students often conceive of learning as the acquisition of correct information, but they may not know what it means to take an active role in the process beyond rote memorization and recall. The classic definition of active learning comes from Bonwell and Eison (1991): active learning is "involving students in doing things and thinking about what they are doing" (p. 2). The Active Learning Site (http://www.active-learning-site.com) maintained by Bonwell contains a wealth of ideas. More in-depth examinations of active learning focus on the challenge of getting students to construct their own learning. The best teachers, according to Bain (2004), "believe that students must learn the facts *while* learning to use them to make decisions about what they understand or what they should do . . . [Such instructors] teach 'the facts' in a rich context of problems, issues, and questions" (p. 29).

You can include a description of your expectations for student initiative in your syllabus. If contributing to class discussion is important, explain that doing so helps you ascertain how students are processing the information they are reading. Asking students to bring prepared responses to questions helps them arrive in class prepared to present their ideas. Working in pairs, then in small groups, and, finally, in a whole-class discussion may be a strategy for coaching students to participate in increasingly larger groups. If critical thinking, problem solving, and inquiry are part of your course, tell students that they will be asked to consider multiple viewpoints and conflicting values and to imagine, analyze, and evaluate alternative positions on issues or solutions to problems. Consult Silberman

(1996) for a compilation of over one hundred active learning strategies that can be adapted for classroom use across the disciplines.

It is especially important to describe what students can expect from you as their teacher. Convey your multiple roles: content expert, formal authority, socializing agent, facilitator, role model, experienced learner, resource consultant, coach, and counselor. Emphasizing and modeling a learning-centered approach discourages students from resisting the work and responsibility that accompanies learning.

Helps Students Assess Their Readiness for Your Course

What are the prerequisites for your course? In your syllabus, tell students what they should already know and what skills they should have mastered before taking your course. This knowledge allows them to realistically assess their readiness. Your syllabus can provide information about the challenges students will face, the assumed skill level, the skills they will build on, and the skills they will learn during your course.

When did students complete these prerequisites? Certainly, you should ask students to provide this information, perhaps on a student information form or data sheet collected the first day of class. In addition, first-day-of-class exercises and activities that require students to demonstrate this knowledge can provide assessment data for you and for your students. Some faculty offer diagnostic quizzes or knowledge surveys (Nuhfer & Knipp, 2003). Some faculty include self-assessment tools and learning contracts to assist students with this process. When a syllabus includes information about institutional offices and Web resources that all students can tap for academic support, you are sending a message that seeking help is a wise behavior, rather than a remedial one.

Sets the Course in a Broader Context for Learning

Your syllabus can provide a perspective that allows students to see instructors in your discipline as active and experienced learners engaged in inquiry in their professional fields or disciplines. Many students are unaware that instructors are involved in research and creative professional activity beyond the classroom; they often regard them simply as transmitters of knowledge and skills.

You can encourage your students to approach the learning situation as apprentice learners in a community of scholars. You can help them see you and other faculty as experienced, active learners who can provide expert guidance about general and specialized knowledge of content and practice in your field.

Your syllabus can provide information that shows students how your course fits within the discipline or profession, the general program of study, and their own educational plans. You can make students aware that every discipline or field has its unique way of knowing. "Doing physics," for example, differs radically from the kind of interpretation required to explicate poems in a literature class. You can encourage students to approach the discipline as ethnographic field-workers who want to understand its social and intellectual practices. Assure them that you will guide them while they learn how to use the characteristic tools and modes of inquiry, patterns of explanation, discourse practices, and types of artifacts that are valued in and produced by their field.

Provides a Conceptual Framework

Your syllabus can support major ideas, topics, and factual information. Include in it questions or issues for students to think about that range from major issues or key questions in the discipline to the meaning of a significant passage in a course reading (Bean, 1996). Place the ideas in the context of current or local events or news so that students see the relevance of the topics to their everyday lives. Such frameworks will help students organize information and focus their learning.

Describes Available Learning Resources

You can list campus resources—such as libraries, reserve desks, reading rooms, laboratories, learning centers, computer clusters, and studios—that students may use (including such resources' locations, availability, and policies) as well as any information concerning the location and use of aids such as CDs, DVDs, poster printing, and copy services. You may also note the locations of specific books and videos and the URLs of various wikis and blogs.

Communicates the Role of Technology in the Course

Computers, computer networks, and new technologies increase our ability to access information and communicate with each other. Technology offers faculty and students working tools that can be used to enhance their thinking; plan and revise learning goals; monitor and reflect on their progress; set up and access their own personal knowledge files; share a common database; build their own database; use a spreadsheet; run statistical software; keep a journal and write, illustrate, and revise texts; and build files for research or a portfolio. New technologies such as podcasting, blogs, or wikis offer resource tools for direct instruction with tutorials or lectures and for research and presentation assignments. Some instructors use more sophisticated resources such as YouTube or Second Life, with some instructional "pitfalls" to consider. Using new technology may come easily to some students, but that technology's application to instruction may not be as apparent. Take time to introduce students to how you intend to use technology, and steer students to campus supports so that they can learn new applications (Windham, 2007).

Electronic discussion boards offer a practical way to interact with your students and a creative way to enrich the content and process goals of a course (Bozik & Tracey, 2002). You can use discussion boards to post assignments, comment on classwork or labwork, and important class information; students can use them to post questions to you and other students and to participate in discussions outside class. Worrall and Kline (2002) found it necessary to create separate discussion threads for content-related exchanges and for informal chatting about the course. If you require students to contribute a certain number of thoughtful comments to an online discussion, be sure to give them in the syllabus or elsewhere examples of acceptable and unacceptable comments, and require that they collect and submit evidence of their contributions to you. If you require that students use grammatically correct English in e-mail messages to you and to peers and in their contributions to online discussions, be sure to explain such netiquette. Course management systems allow documents to be prepared, sent, received, read, and reviewed by the recipient or by all recipients at convenient times. Be sure to inform students of how soon they can expect your reply to an e-mail or to an online posting. Since Millennials may expect an instant response, they will find informative a guideline in the syllabus that indicates, for example, your plan to respond "within forty-eight hours, but not during the weekends."

Studies have shown that students benefit from environments that encourage collaborative and cooperative learning (See the earlier discussion around the NSSE and student engagement). The Web and groupware (such as Lotus Notes and Microsoft Exchange) provide opportunities for asynchronous collaboration (i.e., participants can share work that they do at different times and from different places). Networked writing environments encourage students to write more and learn from each other (Byington, 2002). Online discussion groups can foster fuller participation from students who may not participate in face-to-face classroom environments (Polyson, Saltzberg, & Godwin-Jones, 1996).

Can Provide Difficult-to-Obtain Reading Materials

Sometimes cutting-edge courses must be developed before comprehensive literature is available on a topic. The syllabus for such a course can include copies of articles you want your students to read, as well as supplemental information not found in course texts. You can include materials that expand on, synthesize, and facilitate critical reflection on issues presented during formal instruction. You might include materials that address issues not covered by class presentations or present questions from other points of view. When you use the syllabus in this way, be certain that you obtain necessary copyright clearances for reading selections. Of course, making these resources available through a course management system is far more efficient than printing them as syllabus attachments. Your syllabus, however, can provide URLs to new materials that are not available in print or that are more easily accessed via the Web. Some university libraries will support an electronic course retrieval site for faculty and students.

Can Improve the Effectiveness of Student Note Taking

Good, carefully written notes are a significant resource for active learning. Active thinkers keep notebooks and journals of ideas from readings, lectures, presentations, and their own ruminations about topics. Most students do not learn good note-taking skills in high school. Thus, it is important to help students improve the quality of this form of writing. You may want to include outlines that provide an orientation to lecture and presentation topics, making it clear what you want students to remember and giving them room for their own interpretations of and elaborations on the material. Noyd (2004) has developed a wonderfully interactive strategy called "notetakers" as an antidote to "death by PowerPoint," which occurs when instructors provide all notes to students, usually through a course management system, and, by doing so, discourage class attendance. Notetakers are partial outlines of course lectures that include opportunities for work during class. Students complete some exercises individually and solve other course-related problems in pairs. This strategy actively engages them in completing their notes. If you adopt Noyd's strategy, be sure to include an example of a notetaker in your syllabus. You may also want to include study techniques that are specific to your course. In this way, the contents of the syllabus will help organize and focus student note taking and learning. Resources that help students acquire tools for learning are abundant. Consult supports in texts written by Dembo (2004), Downing (2005), and Heiman and Slomianko (2003), who also offer online supports (see http://www.learningtolearn.com).

Can Include Material That Supports Learning Outside the Classroom

Much learning can and should take place outside the classroom if you deliberately structure your class to build on deep learning principles (Rhem, 1994). Assign homework that gets students into the knowledge base in a motivating way and then use that homework during class time to capitalize on student-student interactions and active learning. Following the principles of cooperative learning (Millis & Cottell, 1998) will make these activities more structured and focused. For example, you might give students a one-page (or shorter) writing assignment that asks them to support, reject, or modify the thesis or claims in the reading which they then discuss in class. Even fairly simple homework assignments such as completing a graphic organizer (a way of visually depicting and connecting learning) such as a Pro-Con-Caveat Grid can help students focus. This homework tool is simply a three-part table that students bring to class and use for subsequent discussion. It asks them to identify (in boxes to encourage brevity, but also critical thinking) the reasons why an action should be adopted, the reasons why it shouldn't, and the extra things that might be considered before making the decision. You can also transform student study time outside class by providing strategies in your syllabus that help students interact more critically with the textbook, supplemental readings, or other work and better prepare them for class. You can also provide self-check assignments that allow students to monitor their progress. For fourteen ways to promote learning outside class, see Hobson's 2004 IDEA paper on this topic at http://www.idea.ksu.edu.

Key research suggests that students do not intuitively know how to study for different disciplines or how to monitor their progress as they master material. You can help students understand how an assignment relates to a topic and why that is meaningful within the context of the course (Bransford et al., 2000). You can also help them understand that their efforts to prepare for class have a strong relationship to their success with assignments and to their outcomes in the course (Svinicki, 2004; Tagg 2003). Thus, when designing a syllabus, consider how you can provide these supports for motivation and learning.

Can Serve as a Learning Contract

As an agreement that defines mutual obligations between instructor and students, your syllabus also speaks for your college or university. On some campuses, the office of the general counsel, the campus's legal experts, cautions against referring to a syllabus as a contract. It's a good idea to learn whether that is the case on your campus before you use the legal term *contract* in discussions of the syllabus with your students. However the terminology is regarded, your syllabus conveys how you meet your teaching responsibilities and how students learn new content and learning strategies as they also begin to value the tools of inquiry, lifelong learning, respect, ethical thinking, and citizenship (Colby, Ehrlich, Beaumont, & Stephens, 2003; Rocheleau & Speck, 2007). The syllabus is your vehicle for conveying that how you have planned the term aligns with the goals of the program and campus. Its messages reflect the values, ideals, and beneficence that are central to higher education. On some campuses, the language employed to convey policies related to, for example, academic honesty, disability access, and civility is standardized.

Such standardized language protects you and the university when students complain about an instructional strategy or requirement or challenge your grading and evaluation decisions. Because the syllabus discloses course requirements thoroughly and conveys policies with ample specificity, two ends are accomplished (Rocheleau & Speck, 2007). First, students know what they have to do to achieve success in the course. Second, academic leaders (chairs, deans, administrators) will be able to depend on your syllabus to defend and protect you—that is, to support your decisions should a student's challenge lead to a grievance. Legal defense provides a grave reason to be sure that you are familiar with institutional policies regarding attendance, examinations, drop/adds, course withdrawals, learning and behavioral disabilities, academic integrity, returning students' work, modifying grades, and ensuring that a syllabus is on file in the department office. Equipped with an understanding of the myriad ways a learning-centered syllabus can function, you can begin to use it in your course.

Using a Learning-Centered Syllabus

As the term begins, it is important to create opportunities for your students to familiarize themselves with the syllabus. Traditionally, faculty used the first day of class *solely* to introduce and thoroughly review the syllabus. With learning-centered practices, many of our colleagues are reconsidering this tradition. They do, of course, distribute the syllabus on day one, but, for several reasons, they may not spend the entire class time reviewing it. Many faculty, for example, want to send a message as the term begins that class time is precious; thus, a focus on learning activities begins on day one. In addition to an engaging content-related activity, faculty might also assess prior knowledge, gather students' reasons for taking the course, or discover their expectations for learning. Creating new first-day traditions can counteract the low attendance patterns prevalent when students believe that "all we do on the first day is get the syllabus and then class is dismissed." This mind-set dismisses the importance of both the syllabus and attendance. By focusing on learning activities from the moment class begins, faculty emphasize the value of attendance and its link to learning.

How can you send this message early on? If you are using an online course management system such as Blackboard or WebCampus, post the course syllabus in advance of the first day of class with an announcement or an assignment requiring students to come prepared to discuss the syllabus. The announcement may also alert students to your intent of using the full class period constructively. It is a good idea to post—through the most convenient medium—an agenda before students arrive and you can also announce a schedule of activities—including a discussion or exercise involving the syllabus—as the class convenes. Although on many campuses you can assume that students have access to campus e-mail and course management system accounts, you will want to determine on the first day of class that all students have access to the same resources. On campuses where some students may be unfamiliar with essential technology supports, you may need to review the technology options as class begins and identify peer mentors in class or point newcomers to campus offices that can help familiarize them with these tools.

You may want to use some specific strategies to ensure that students read the syllabus thoroughly. You could, for example, ask your students to review the syllabus outside class and respond to it in an essay by identifying your role, elaborating on their roles, and raising any questions. Responses can be sent electronically by e-mail or submitted through the course management system so that you can review them before the next class meeting. If your syllabus is available online, ask students to review this version, noting and responding to the links that are available with a few clicks of the mouse. You might also give a syllabus quiz during the next class. Another strategy is to divide the class into small groups, assigning sections of the syllabus to each and giving each time in class to review and clarify their assigned sections. When the syllabus is discussed later, group members respond as experts to the questions raised about their assigned sections.

Take time during the first week of the term to discuss the various sections of the syllabus. It may be productive to stretch this discussion over two or three class meetings. Emphasize to your students that you have tried to anticipate their learning needs through the syllabus. Thus, it includes not only the content needed to support their learning but also useful information for active, purposeful, and effective learning in the course. Refer them to your teaching philosophy statement, and explain how it is reflected in your course objectives, activities, and requirements. Giving students sufficient time to discuss their respective roles and responsibilities in the course will increase their familiarity and comfort with active learning and with your expectations.

Weimer (2002) echoes this observation and cautions that "student and faculty resistance is all but a guaranteed response to learner-centered teaching" (p. 149). She offers a variety of explanations and suggestions to analyze the resistance you experience and strategies to use in response.

Turning to the syllabus often and throughout the semester encourages students to develop the habit of using it as a reference during the course. Discuss the learning tools that you have included and strategies for their use. If you have included key terms that you will use in discussions or lectures, refer students to those definitions, and encourage them to locate others or to develop their own definitions as they come to understand the terms more clearly and to connect those terms to applied contexts. If you have included tools that are intended to help students take more useful notes or to serve as ground rules for different types of discussion, refer to them at times when they would be most helpful.

Refer to the syllabus when discussing new assignments and identify the course objectives that particular assignments meet. Encourage students to make their own notes, elaborating on those that you have made for them. Allow time for discussing assignments. What are the learning objectives for this assignment? How much freedom do students have to learn in their own way? How are the criteria for evaluation set? Are the criteria clear enough that students will be able to measure their own progress? How do you anticipate the work will proceed, and at what points will you help students assess their progress? Is there a place in the assignment to develop assessment criteria together with your students? Oral or group presentations offer reasonable starting points to identify assessment criteria; everyone can contribute presentation skills that engage an audience.

When approaching tests, examinations, or other assessment tools, allow time for questions and suggestions about assessment. Make available examples of concrete learning outcomes that have already been evaluated by the criteria to be used. Including exemplary but realistic examples of other students' accomplishments can clarify your expectations for students and will often inspire students' efforts toward their own work (Weimer, 2002; Wlodkowski & Ginsberg, 1995). Composition faculty routinely offer past examples of good and poor papers that students assess with a well-constructed rubric. As students' proficiency increases, their analyses of the quality differences may lead them to develop the assessment criteria for a future product. Critiquing other compositions helps students form a realistic picture of what is expected of them in the paper they are currently writing.

You might want to think of your syllabus as a negotiable agreement, a well-considered plan in which you are willing to reinvent some of the structure according to the students and situation you find in your class (Weimer 2002; Wlodkowski & Ginsberg, 1995). A questionnaire at midterm or other appropriate time can elicit useful information, help you determine whether revisions are required, and reinforce your expectations for students' responsibility in shaping their education and your interest in their accomplishments. A half-page sheet works well with the prompts of "What should I stop doing/start doing/continue doing?" If your campus offers a midsemester online feedback survey, take advantage of this resource to learn how students are experiencing the course and interpreting the strategies you have put in place. If not, design your own survey, and ask a student to administer it and collect the data so that the rest of the class is assured that responses are anonymous. Small-group instructional diagnosis (SGID) is another tool used to assess students' class experiences during the semester when instructors can respond to the feedback (Black, 1998; Redmond & Clark, 1982; Wulff & Nyquist, 1986). In SGID, a trained colleague, TA, or consultant from the campus teaching and learning center uses two questions to interview the class and build consensus with the students' responses: what is helping your learning in this class, and what could improve your learning in this class? The process takes about forty-five minutes and concludes with three or four recommendations for each question, which the interviewer conveys to the instructor.

Your learning-centered syllabus can be a dynamic document that becomes an integral part of your course, that encourages and supports student engagement and interaction, and that leads to the active, purposeful, effective learning that you want to promote.

Part II

Examples

TO HELP YOU compose or revise your syllabus with a learning-centered perspective, we have provided examples of sections that you might want to include. In general, however, the syllabus should do the following things:

- Describe the course, including its goals and objectives

- Outline the structure of the course and its significance within the general program of study (particularly any nontraditional aspects of it that may be new to the students)

- Discuss the obligations that you and the students share for learning outcomes, for the activities and processes of learning, and for respecting the behavioral codes valued by you, the program, and the campus

- Give a clear explanation of assessment and evaluation practices—that is, how you will provide feedback on how well students have been achieving and meeting the course goals and objectives

- Provide critical logistic and procedural information about what will happen, when it will happen, and where it will happen, including activities and assignments

In describing the various sections, we have drawn from materials from a broad range of institutions and disciplines, being careful to include traditional face-to-face courses, hybrid or blended courses, and online examples. The examples are primarily from undergraduate offerings but also include some graduate courses. While the examples were not necessarily developed within a framework of learning-centeredness, each contributes something to a learning-centered perspective. We hope that they will assist you in designing a learning-centered syllabus that will fit the specific conditions and circumstances in which you and your students work.

Checklist

What you include in your syllabus will be determined by your students' needs, the type of course you are offering, and the rationale underlying that course. This checklist can serve as a guide when you prepare your syllabus. Examples of each of these items follow.

- Table of contents
- Instructor information
- Student information form
- Letter to the students or teaching philosophy statement
- Purpose of the course
- Course description
- Course objectives
- Readings
- Resources
- Course calendar
- Course requirements
- Policies and expectations: Attendance, late papers, missed tests, class behaviors, and civility
- Policies and expectations: Academic honesty, disability access, and safety
- Evaluation
- Grading procedures
- How to succeed in this course: Tools for study and learning

Table of Contents

If you are one of the rare instructors who organizes your syllabus in the form of an extended course manual, then you will likely have a cover page and a table of contents. Because students often read a syllabus in sections based on their immediate needs, it is important to demarcate material and to make items easy for them to locate.

The way that you organize your manual depends on the content of your course. You may decide to deal with the course as a whole, or it may work better to divide the course into units (e.g., objectives, assignments, evaluations).

Example: Table of Contents

Readings...2

eCollege...2

Course Requirements and Assignments..2

Class Preparation and Participation..2

Writing and the Writing Center..2

Philosophical Traditions..3

Philosophy Teams, Philosopher Study Groups, Philosopher
Roundtables..3

Philosophy Challenges..4

Ethics..5

Ethics Challenges...5

Final Portfolio...7

Grading Criteria..8

Course Schedule...11

Statement on Disability Services at TCU..11

Standards Covered...12

Course Policies...12

Adapted from EDEC 41113: Learner-Centered Foundations of Education, *Texas Christian University, M. Francyne Huckaby, 2006.*

Instructor Information

The syllabus provides a record of the course instructor so that students know who you are and how to contact you. Students should always know where, when, and how to reach their instructors. Instructor accessibility is important to students, who may also expect—unless you provide parameters—24/7 responses. If the course includes multiple instructors and/or TAs, accessibility to the entire team is important. Consider introducing yourself in the syllabus by identifying your educational history and your research interests. In the examples that follow, you can see how some colleagues also offer students glimpses into their hobbies and personalities.

Example 1: Instructor Information
Contacting Karl Smith and Vaughan Voller

Karl Smith is quite easy to contact outside of office hours if you persist. If you're in the neighborhood, try knocking on the door (236 Civil Engineering). If there's no answer, leave a message on the notepad, and I'll phone. Try phoning me at 625-0305; if I don't answer (I'm either in a conference, on the phone, or out of my office), leave voice mail, and I'll return your call.

Send me e-mail (probably the most reliable way to reach me), and I'll respond. I read my e-mail regularly during the day and almost every evening at about 10:00 P.M., and I will reply promptly. If you want to meet in person and you're unable to meet during office hours, please contact me and make an appointment.

Vaughan Voller will be in 167 Civil Engineering. His phone number is 625–0765. BUT e-mail works best—volle001@umn.edu

Adapted from UHC 1105: Building Models to Solve Engineering Problems, *University Honors College, University of Minnesota, Karl Smith and Vaughan Voller, Summer, 2003.*

Example 2: Instructor Information

Instructor: Ray Pfeiffer, PhD, CPA, Associate Professor

Office address: 355 School of Management

Internet address: pfeiffer@acctg.umass.edu

Web URL: http://intra.som.umass.edu/pfeiffer (includes course Web site!)

Office phone: 413–545–5653

Office mailbox: Located in room 230, School of Management

Office hours: M, T, W, and Th 11:00–12:00 or by appointment

Education: Stroudsburg High School (Stroudsburg, PA), 1983; Moravian College (Bethlehem, PA)—BA (Accounting), 1987; University of North Carolina at Chapel Hill—PhD (Accounting), 1994

Work experience: Associate Professor, University of Massachusetts 2000–present; Assistant Professor, University of Massachusetts, 1994–2000; Audit Staff, Deloitte & Touche, 1987–1990; Staff Accountant (Intern), Stone, Cyphers, McCoy, and DeAngelo, summer 1996. Certified Public Accountant, Pennsylvania and North Carolina.

Research interests: Financial reporting issues, financial reporting regulation, firms' accounting and disclosure choices, and stock market participants' use of financial statement information

Outside interests: Playing piano (mostly jazz), arranging/composing and listening to music, playing tennis, skiing, cooking, film, politics, and college basketball

Contacting me: Feel free to call me at the office, e-mail me, or stop by my office. I check my e-mail regularly, but please do not expect a response by e-mail after normal business hours.

Adapted from ACCTG 322: Financial Reporting II, *University of Massachusetts Amherst, Ray Pfeiffer, 2006.*

Example 3: Instructor Information (with Deliberate Humor)

Responsible for Course:

Name: Ronald A. Berk, PhD, CNN, MTV, DNA, Professor

Office: Room 433

Phone: 410–955–8212

E-mail: rberk@son.jhmi.edu

Office Hours:

MWF: 7:00 A.M.–3:00 P.M.

TTH: 9:00 P.M.–2:30 A.M.

Open all legal and illegal holidays.

Closed Sunday for mental repairs.

Adapted from NR100.513.0101 Inferential Biostatistics, *Johns Hopkins School of Nursing, Ron Berk, 2005.*

Student Information Form

There are a variety of strategies to ensure that you have instant access to students' contact information. An old standby is to distribute index cards during the first week of the semester and ask students to record their name, e-mail address, mailing address, and telephone numbers. An alternative is to include in the syllabus a student information page that students can complete and return during the next class. Such a form can also be uploaded to the course management system as a first assignment to complete and submit online. The example that follows can be adapted to suit the particular needs or requirements of any course. It was developed by Margaret Cohen of the University of Missouri–St. Louis, and it is available online from the Center for Teaching and Learning at http://www.umsl.edu/services/ctl/instr_support/tchng_res.html.

Example: Student Information Form

Please complete this information page, and return it to me at the next class meeting. I will use this information to plan the semester, to get to know you, and to contact you by mail, phone, or e-mail, if the need arises. I will not share this information with anyone without your consent.

Semester: _____

Reference number: _____

Name: _____

Student ID#: _____

Address: _____   Apt.: _____

City: _____   State: _____   Zip code: _____

Contact me by phone at . . . Home: _____   Work: _____

Mobile: _____   Other: _____

My campus e-mail address: _____

Indicate the semester and year in which you completed these course prerequisites:

[Insert course name and number]: _____

[Insert course name and number]: _____

Identify the degree program or certificate program you are in: _____

How many credit hours have you completed to date on campus? _____

Explain why you are taking this course and how it fits into your degree or certificate program: _____

What are your expectations for the course? _____

Briefly describe related experiences or courses that are relevant to this course: _____

If you require special accommodations, indicate that and please be sure to meet with me soon: _____

Letter to the Students or Teaching Philosophy Statement

Including a letter to the students in the syllabus enhances the personal nature of the course, can help relieve student discomfort, and can set a conversational tone for your course. Some faculty members send a welcoming letter to students before the first class meeting, an option increasingly available through course management systems. This letter can include your teaching philosophy statement as a way of helping students become acquainted with you as a professional.

Collins (1997) reminds us of the particular value of this communication to first-generation students, who may feel that higher education is a closed system that doesn't welcome "outsiders." He states, "To the newcomers who are our students . . . the norms and ground rules of higher education are neither clear nor valued" (p. 1). Thus, anything we can do to help all our students feel comfortable in our courses—such as letters to students and open disclosures of how and why we do what we do (i.e., philosophies)—goes a long way toward motivating them to succeed. Including your teaching philosophy statement clarifies what you value about the instructional process and lays a foundation that justifies why you've organized the course as you have.

Example 1: Letter to the Students

I am so pleased that you are in my Composition I class. Although you may look on this class as merely a stepping-stone to furthering your education, I hope you realize as the class proceeds that you will be learning important lifelong skills that will help you in other classes, your career, and your personal life. This class takes place in a computer classroom, so you will also be learning important computer skills.

During this class, you will have an opportunity to practice writing for different situations and audiences. You will learn more about your process of writing and what strategies work best for you. You will learn to share your ideas with others, discovering along the way how much you know and what others' perspectives are. If you keep an open mind and a willingness to participate, you will be pleasantly pleased at how your writing improves. This course does require a commitment from you: a responsibility to attend class and to be prepared with assignments on time. My expectations of you are high because I know what is possible.

I base many of my teaching principles on the theories behind a learning-centered class included in the Seven Principles for Good Practice in Undergraduate Education (see Chickering & Gamson, 1987). So that you will better understand these principles I have listed them below:

Good Practice Encourages Student-Faculty Contact

Student-faculty contact promotes motivation and involvement. I want you to know that I am available to you during my office hours, in the Writing Center, and by phone and e-mail. I cannot know you are having difficulty in the class unless you tell me.

Good Practice Encourages Cooperation among Students

Good learning is collaborative and social, not competitive and isolated. We will be working together as a team, and teamwork requires cooperation from all of a team's members. That means good listening skills as well as good speaking skills.

Good Practice Encourages Active Learning

Students learn most when they are engaged in their own learning by writing, by relating the information to past knowledge, and by applying it to their daily lives. I am not a lecturer. I will explain certain new strategies or functions and then let you practice applying them, asking questions as you experiment, discover, and create.

Good Practice Gives Prompt Feedback

Students need frequent opportunities to test their competence, reflect on what they have learned and need to learn, and assess themselves. I plan to return papers promptly so that you may learn from your mistakes, correct them, and eliminate them on the next assignment.

Good Practice Emphasizes Time on Task

Students need help in time management, and the instructor can be the best model of that principle. I will stick to the task and use our time wisely; I expect you to do the same.

Good Practice Communicates High Expectations

Expecting students to perform well becomes a self-fulfilling prophecy when teachers and institutions hold high expectations of themselves and make extra efforts.

Good Practice Respects Diverse Talents and Ways of Learning

Students come to the classroom with various learning styles and backgrounds. Providing opportunities for all students to show their talents and to learn in ways most comfortable to them enriches the classroom.

Let's have a fun and rewarding semester together.

Best wishes and good luck,

Ellen Mohr

Adapted from Composition 121, *Johnson County Community College, Ellen Mohr, 2006.*

Example 2: Teaching Philosophy Statement

My goals as a teacher are to inspire my students to learn and to challenge them to reach their fullest potential. To help my students achieve these goals, I embrace the following philosophy regarding teaching.

1. I believe that my purpose as a teacher goes beyond the teaching of accounting. It is equally important to help students to grow as people, to support their intellectual and professional development, to challenge their assumptions, and to expand their worldviews. I believe that I succeed as a teacher when my students are inspired to teach themselves. Ideally, my role is to appeal to each individual's inner intellectual curiosity, which I believe is the most valuable educational resource.

2. I believe in challenging my students to reach very high standards of performance and in providing them with the resources they need to reach those standards. I believe that just about anybody can learn just about anything in such an environment.

3. I take my role in the learning process very seriously. I want my students to know that I am personally invested in their success or failure because I care very deeply that they learn.

4. I believe that the most important element of learning is building structure. Without a framework, students are unlikely to internalize facts, rules, ideas, and techniques. With a framework and the ability to build their own frameworks, students can become critical thinkers and thus more effective learners and professionals.

5. I believe that I should continuously improve my teaching skills and the content of my courses. This includes keeping the material current with the state of the art in the academic literature and in practice; finding new ways to make the material appeal to students' curiosity; making efficient use of class time; and introducing new pedagogical tools that recognize diverse learning styles and enhance my ability to reach my students.

Love of teaching was my first inspiration to pursue an academic career. In my eleven and a half years of teaching, I realize that I love it even more than I thought I would. My work as a teacher is a crucial part of my contribution to my profession, to the university, and to society. As such, the privilege to teach continues to be an enormous source of personal reward and inspiration for me.

Adapted from ACCTG 322: Financial Reporting II, *University of Massachusetts Amherst, Ray Pfeiffer, 2006.*

Example 3: Teaching Philosophy Statement
My Rules of the Road

1. I believe too many classroom rules get in the way of good teaching and good learning.

2. Optimal teaching is not blissful teaching. It is adjustable, flexible, and dynamic teaching. The good teacher has to be a master at impromptu, at making split-second decisions, at quick thinking.

3. WARNING!!! WARNING!!!! WARNING!!! If you are the type of person who needs to talk about EVERYTHING in EVERY chapter of our text . . . then you will be frustrated by this course!!! We simply cannot cover EVERYTHING and still practice our skills. You have absolute permission to stop me if we get too far off track, but sometimes it is necessary to go down unanticipated paths!

4. I can't just *go* into a class; I have to *get* into it.

5. You too will get out of this class knowledge and understanding based on what you put into it.

6. Teaching is something I do *with* students, not something I do *to* them.

7. What knowledge do I have that is greater and more powerful and more effective than caring, kindness, and commitment to students' learning?

8. A class day is wasted if I haven't smiled and laughed with you.

9. Students can hold me spellbound if I hold myself open to their promise.

10. Consistent teaching does not mean always doing it the same way. Many are the times that consistency means remembering to forget.

11. If I want to be free and happy in teaching, I have to sacrifice routine and boredom.

12. Give a damn! Care! This class won't be worth our time if we aren't both invested.

13. I will focus on the student and his/her learning and worry about the subject and teaching later.

14. I don't enter the classroom expecting students to fail. I expect them to learn and succeed. I try and help each student expect that of him/herself.

15. This class is a "gathering of ones," a group of diverse, individual, sacred human beings—I strive to treat them as such.

16. Every student starts with a clean slate. I strive not to judge students by anything other than their contribution to today's class.

17. I care about every student. It's OK to be disappointed in or even frustrated with their lack of effort or success, but I will not stop caring about them as people.

18. The three Rs don't mean a thing if they don't make the student a better person.

Adapted from MGT-300-02: Principles of Management, *Saint Louis University, Mike Shaner, Spring 2006. Louis Schmier originated the Rules of the Road concept for history courses he teaches at Valdosta State University in Georgia.*

Purpose of the Course

This next section of the syllabus—the purpose of the course—should focus on why the course exists, how it fits into the larger curriculum, and for whom it was designed. This section of the syllabus gives you an opportunity to discuss "course alignment"—that is, how the course meshes with others in the program and with the university's overall mission. If students understand from the start your intended goals, then you can discuss those goals in depth and pursue them together. Showing how the course is relevant to students' success on campus and to their future career goals can motivate students by piquing their interest in the course's purpose.

Example 1: Purpose of the Course

We now live in a global community and have increasing contact with people of other cultures. Cross-cultural encounters bring complexity to our lives. They also bring the opportunity to see ourselves and others with new lenses and to embark on uncharted voyages of adventure. The metaphors, then, for this course are that of *seeing* and taking a *journey*.

The course itself is not rigidly charted. We have goals, themes, topics, resources, and activities in mind but also welcome detours and lengthened visits in places we together find worthy of exploration.

Adapted from Seminar on Intercultural Interpretations, *Duquesne University, Cynthia Lennox and Laurel Willingham-McLain, Fall 2005.*

Example 2: Purpose of the Course

"We need a return to family values" is a theme we hear frequently in the media, as the traditional model of the nuclear family seems increasingly fragile in the rapidly changing world of contemporary America. This formulation of the problem leaves unanswered the questions "What is a family?" and "What do we value about it?" Answering these questions is not easy because, as the economic and social functions that families fulfill have changed throughout American history, the forms taken by the family have multiplied and changed. The American family could be a single parent with children, a family in poverty, a multigenerational household, an adoptive family, a lesbian or gay family, or that traditional nuclear family, which has itself evolved from *Leave It to Beaver* to *Two and a Half Men*.

Together, we will critically assess the American family as a social institution, asking questions such as these: What are the functions of a family? How does the evolution of family forms reflect changes in the functions families have needed to perform? Is it meaningful to speak of a "normal" family? Taught by an economist and a psychologist-lawyer, this class will discuss contributions from literature (*The Color Purple, Oedipus Rex,* and *The Handmaid's Tale*) and popular culture (*Pleasantville* and relevant TV shows), as well as readings from several disciplines that study the family—history, psychology, economics, anthropology, and sociology.

Adapted from The Evolution of the American Family, *St. Lawrence University, Cathy Crosby-Currie and Steve Horwitz, Fall 2006.*

Example 3: Purpose of the Course
Rationale and Requirements for This Course

Each summer I spend time reading about teaching and learning. My courses are influenced as I educate myself further. This summer I spent a good bit of time thinking about *holistic* education—there are many principles to this philosophy of education, but a few are salient to what I propose for you all this semester.

1. Our education should promote growth of the whole person, not solely focus on cognitive development. We espouse such a belief in early childhood education particularly, but as school continues, the concentration is mostly directed at enhancing analytical skills and transferring valued information. Yet, I believe teaching depends on our growth and health not only intellectually but also psychoemotionally and spiritually. Actually, all healthy lives involve growth, awareness, and balance in regard to these three human domains.

2. Education is intensely personal in terms of needs and interests. Our motivations are also the most reliable starting and sustaining agents in our learning. Thus, common curricula are rarely useful at a personal level, even if voluntary. If involuntary, a common curriculum is dependent on extrinsic motivators and modestly successful, at best. Compliance is the best behavior we can possibly extract from a class. Moreover, each of us has different needs or interests in regard to the three domains—thus, whatever I ask you to do for this class will be personalized and/or built on choices.

3. Learning/growth involves personal responsibility—that's the counterpoint to having choice and guiding learning by personal goals and interests. You must reflect, plan, act, and assess. If you can identify learning goals

or opportunities, then you have the obligation of pursuing and achieving them. At some point, you must choose to own your learning.

4. For all of us who won't be isolates or hermits, education does have social implications. We need to acquire capacities relevant to social living, to living in a socially desirable and contributing manner. We who will teach should be especially aware of this aspect of the educational process. Moreover, as we are a social species, we learn better those curricula that are inherently social (e.g., it's easier to learn baseball with others than alone). This is not to say all learning ought to be social.

5. OK, beyond the holism and progressivism that I want to embed in this course, we inherit a couple of duties or constraints that shape the course. This course is a Writing Emphasis course. The policy requirements that a WE course must follow may be found on the TCU Web site.

Adapted from EDSE/EDMS 30013: Professional Roles and Responsibilities, *Texas Christian University, Mike Sacken, 2006.*

Course Description

A strong course description early in the syllabus can generate student interest by providing a stimulating overview of the course, including its content, value, and the philosophical assumptions behind it. You can increase students' enthusiasm and motivation by emphasizing the relevance of the course. You will also want the description to reflect your values and attitudes. This section of the syllabus provides students with an explanation of how the course will be conducted (e.g., through lectures, small-group discussion, project teams, field experiences, simulations). Check to see whether your campus or department policy requires that you include in the syllabus the published bulletin description of the course. If so, include your own description to augment the formal one.

Example 1: Course Description

What makes us tick? What happens when that ticking goes wrong? How can we help? In fact, *who* should help—family, society, medical doctors, clinicians? What theories best inform clinical practice? *How* are theories put into play by therapists or clinicians? Clinical psychology is the field of study in which we attempt to answer these questions. Clinical psychology is primarily a profession, based on a relevant knowledge base. Both areas—the practice and the knowledge base—will be the focus of the course. In this course, you will be learning as much as possible about the knowledge base concerning dysfunctional human behavior. You will also be learning about the methods and skills that a clinical psychologist uses to accomplish the goals of treatment, in both a clinical internship setting and a classroom setting.

This course will rely heavily on three types of "texts" to teach you about clinical psychology's knowledge content, methods, and skills:

1. A textbook that should provide you with content (theory, history, and general practices of clinical psychology)

2. Your community placement

3. Current publications regarding clinical practice (journal articles and professional publications)

I regard your community internship placement as a kind of text because the experiences, observations, and reflections that stem from your placement will serve as a separate *source of knowledge* for you that cannot be replicated in any formal written way. You will share some of your experiences with others in our class, to share and deepen the learning that you gain from your placement.

Human behavior is the focus of all three "texts" described above. Our goals in examining human behavior are not only to try to understand the roots of that behavior but also to understand how behavior becomes dysfunctional and how that behavior can be changed back into a more functional, satisfactory behavior. The course will use *reading, speaking, listening,* and *writing* as the primary skills to master these ambitious course goals. Of course, you already know how to read, speak, etc. Clinical psychologists, however, use particular rules, customs, and habits when they speak and listen in a clinical mode. These habits are not easy to acquire, but you can begin to learn about them, and practice them in a limited way, in this course.

Adapted from PSYCH 443: Introduction to Clinical Psychology, *St. Lawrence University, Pamela Thacher, Fall 2006.*

Example 2: Course Description

We live in a world in which decisions are made according to research. Based on the findings of all types of studies, we choose foods, universities, majors, and laws to make our lives better and safer. Because of this, two issues are very important. We need to distinguish between good and bad research, and we need to be able to conduct research to make persuasive arguments. This course is designed to help you in both of these areas so that you can be a discriminating consumer and a responsible producer of information. This information will be valuable to you in both your classes and your everyday life. Your communication classes require that you understand the research process to read, comprehend, and design communication research. Moreover, in the future you will probably be required to conduct some form of research to determine whether a new product is working, whether there is a need for more personnel, or how to best talk your boss into a raise. This course will help prepare you for all these goals.

Adapted from CMMA 280-01: Communication Research, *Saint Louis University, Paaige Turner, Fall 2006.*

Example 3: Course Description

"Once upon a time and far away," notes Amy McClure, "children's books were perceived as simple things, concerned with naughty little rabbits, perplexed toy bears, and fairy princesses." Books for children and adolescents are no longer simple, if they ever were (go ask Alice!). HUM 499 assumes that such books deserve careful study, demanding the same skills of critical thinking and analysis brought to any literature course. The work will be examined from three perspectives: literature, art, and ethical values. Cadets will view these books holistically, noting the creative ways in which authors and illustrators combine to produce works of art that should be viewed from the perspective of values.

This course will be grounded in the universal values of a work—*The Odyssey*—which was not originally intended for young people, but is now widely taught in public high schools. We will thus look at *Charlotte's Web* from the perspective of friendship, loyalty, and sacrifice. *Sounder,* a mini-epic featuring a boy's journey of discovery to find his father, will offer themes exemplified by quotations from Montaigne: "Cowardice is the mother of cruelty" and "Only the unwise think that what has changed is dead." With *I Am the Cheese,* we will go on yet another journey, one filled with betrayal and isolation ("The cheese stands alone"). This genre-based course will provide a history of children's literature but will concentrate primarily on selected works from the twentieth century. The various genres will be explored at all levels through a range of authors and illustrators. Cadets will focus in depth on topics of interest to them through literary analysis/reaction papers and oral presentations complemented by written commentary. They will have an opportunity to explore one particular topic in depth through a capstone final project approved by the instructors. The topic could involve preparing a traditional research paper, exploring ethical issues through several works, or creating an original work, such as writing and illustrating a book.

Adapted from HUM 499: Literature, Art, and Ethics in Books for Children and Young Adults, *United States Air Force Academy, Barbara J. Millis and Pam Chadick, Spring 2004.*

Course Objectives

An important function of your syllabus is to indicate to students their accountability in your course—what they will have to do, and under what conditions. Students should be able to find out where your course leads intellectually and practically, what they will know by the end of the course, what they will be able to do by the end of the course, and how they will be expected to demonstrate what they have learned. Is one of the purposes of the course to improve their problem-solving abilities? Improve their communication skills? Allow them to translate knowledge from one context to another? Why are the goals important, and how will different parts of the course help students accomplish those goals? One way of looking at these objectives is to ask yourself, "What do I want my students to look like at the end of this course? Five years down the road?" Objectives make goals more specific, providing a basic plan for what is to be accomplished and how that should be evaluated in students. In a learning-centered syllabus, objectives describe both the learning processes students will develop and the products of linking those processes with the course content.

You may sometimes combine course objectives with the course description, depending on their complexity and the nature of the course and discipline. Course objectives describing what students should be able to do at the end of the semester usually appear either as a succinct statement or as an outline. They are ideally described with action verbs. Clear objectives can foster a sense of partnership and an awareness that you and your students are working toward the same goals. Objectives provide both a focus and a motivation for learning.

Asking yourself four basic questions can help you formulate and communicate your objectives or goals:

1. What are the student learning outcomes of the course in relation to the overall major or minor degree program or professional accreditation standards?

2. What do you want your students to learn? What are your course objectives?

3. How will you determine that students have accomplished what you set out to help them learn?

4. What activities—whether in-class, out-of-class, or online—will help students meet these learning outcomes?

In other words, how will you evaluate their progress and achievements? What assignments, classroom activities, e-learning assignments, and pedagogical approaches will help them master the specified knowledge, skills, or attitude changes?

Objectives can be written at a course or unit level. They may be of two different types:

1. Concrete statements of what students will be able to do as the result of learning.

2. Open-ended, flexible descriptions of a situation or problem out of which various kinds of learning might arise.

Objectives, then, would be expectations that delimit the direction of the students but do not predefine an end point for their learning or try to guarantee a particular interpretation or outcome. You would let more specific objectives emerge as they are appropriate to an individual student in resolving a particular task. Terminology in this regard is problematic. Education experts tell us that objectives should be measurable, yet many of us have more nebulous outcomes that are difficult to quantify such as developing a sense of civic responsibility or learning to appreciate great works of literature. Thus, the terminology sometimes shifts toward "aims" or "goals."

Example 1: Course Objectives
Instructor Goals
I plan to . . .

1. Develop students' appreciation of selected works of world literature (also film and other art forms) from different times, cultures, and ethical and religious value systems, focusing on comparative examples of the psychological novel

2. Help students relate these works to their lives and help students appreciate the value of liberal arts learning

3. Assist students in analyzing literature and other art forms and reflecting/conversing/writing about them as both individual and collaborative learners

4. Help students develop the process skills of reflection, analysis, synthesis, and evaluation in their reading, writing, and thinking

5. Assist students in developing appropriate modes of inquiry into the study and appreciation of literary art forms, particularly the novel

6. Continue to develop students' critical-thinking and reading skills and ability to engage in reasoned and informed personal and collaborative reflection, conversation, informal online writing, and researched writing, using technology to enhance learning and sharpen their ability to analyze various texts

7. Encourage open, honest, respectful, critical discourse on diverse multicultural issues and topics that derive from course readings and content

Course Goals

After the course, the student should . . .

1. Develop the ability to read, think, converse, and write critically about various literary works from diverse cultures; analyze different examples of the psychological novel; and engage in effective verbal and written discourse about literature and other art and media forms

2. Appreciate the relationship of literature to life

3. Acquire critical skills essential to the understanding of ideas and principles central to humanistic liberal learning, which are outgrowths of the study of important literature

4. Continue to demonstrate appropriate skills of effective research, reading, writing, oral communication, individual and collaborative reflective practice, and implementation of technology for higher-order learning and for mature understanding of diverse types of novels in the genre that is the focus of our course

Course Objectives

To meet the goals, the student will . . .

1. Demonstrate an understanding of various literary works from diverse cultures and how such different texts deal with the central themes of the course and relate to their individual lives

2. Show proficiency in critically reading, analyzing, comparing, researching, evaluating, discussing, and writing about diverse literary works and other art forms and texts and in applying their learning to their individual lives

3. Recognize how different works of world literature and other art forms reflect the characteristics of their times, their places, their authors, and their cultural values

4. Write analytically about the texts we read in both formal and informal assignments, such as short essays, research papers, bibliographies, and electronic threaded discussion postings

5. Demonstrate appropriate methods of research and documented writing and of using information and communication technologies to support learning activities

Course Outcomes
Success will be measured in these ways

In formally written, carefully polished essays; in collaborative projects involving electronic and print search strategies and presentation methods; in bibliographic work; in class discussions; in generous, substantive, reflective engagement in an electronic threaded discussion; and in a comprehensive, reflective learning portfolio, the student will . . .

1. Correctly and successfully discuss various literary elements identified in our readings

2. Compare themes, authors, and technical dimensions of the fiction studied in the course

3. Develop advanced competency in critical thinking, reading, written and oral communication, and the use of technology to enhance learning about diverse texts by writing effective responses to literary topics, by doing traditional and technology-assisted research on such topics, and by participating effectively, both individually and collaboratively, in real and virtual class discussions and reports

Adapted from English 310 N (Honors): The Psychological Novel, *Columbia College, John Zubizarreta, Fall 2006.*

Example 2: Course Objectives

Upon completion of this course, the student should be able to:

1. Define common chemical terms (a detailed list of terms is given in each unit)

2. Solve numerical conversion problems related to chemical principles

3. Identify the basic components of an atom and relate those components to the elements in the periodic table

4. Describe properties of elements based on their position in the periodic table

5. Describe nuclear radiation and nuclear reactions

6. Write the correct formula and name of a chemical compound

7. Diagram electron dot structures for elements and covalent compounds

8. Balance a chemical or nuclear reaction

9. Identify and diagram changes of energy in chemical reactions

10. Name and draw complete or condensed formulas for simple organic compounds

11. Complete and balance organic combustion, addition, amidation, esterification, oxidation, and reduction reactions

12. Recognize basic organic functional groups (a complete list is given in the unit goals)

13. Describe properties of solutions and their formation

14. Complete and balance dissociation, precipitation, ionization, and neutralization reactions

15. Calculate concentration of solutions amount of solvent or solute

16. Determine pH of a solution and classify as acid, base, or neutral

17. Describe the role of buffers in maintaining the pH of a solution

18. Classify carbohydrates and identify isomers

19. Draw the structures of monosaccharides, triglycerides, amino acids, and dipeptides

20. Distinguish between the different structures of proteins

Adapted from CHEM 122: Principles of Chemistry, *Johnson County Community College, Kevin Gratton and Csilla Duneczky, Fall 2005.*

Example 3: Course Objectives

First, I want you to master a set of skills—how to account for and report on transactions involving long-term liabilities, equity, accounting changes, and the statement of cash flows. Often, these skills are the sole focus of courses like this one. However, the business world and the accounting profession continue to change very dramatically, and this has placed additional demands on you as a student.

One such change is the increased prevalence of computer-based accounting systems. Much of the work once done by accounting professionals is now done instead by machines. Accordingly, to add value, today's accounting graduates must possess higher-level skills—the ability to *analyze, synthesize,* and *critically evaluate* information, rather than just know how to *prepare* it. To help you meet this challenge, I strive to make sure you are developing these skills and knowledge that will enable you to become effective decision makers and business advisers, not just number crunchers:

1. You should develop an appreciation for the conceptual framework underlying Generally Accepted Accounting Principles. This includes

developing an understanding of the forces that shape accounting practice and cause it to be consistent and sometimes inconsistent, and learning to recognize common patterns and exceptions to those patterns that exist in accounting practice. It also includes understanding the trade-offs involved in standards setting, the limitations of current accounting standards, and the effects that these trade-offs and limitations have on the quality and content of information that is communicated by financial statements.

2. You should gain an appreciation of firms' abilities and incentives to choose from a wide variety of alternative measurement bases and accounting procedures and the effects that those choices might have on the readers of firms' financial statements. This requires an integrated understanding of business from many dimensions. I also want you to become a sophisticated reader of financial reports who appreciates the subtleties of financial communication and who can read between the lines to draw inferences that lead to good decisions.

3. You should strive to improve your ability to communicate in the language of the discipline, both orally and in writing.

4. You should increase your facility with electronic spreadsheets (e.g., Microsoft Excel) because such skills are increasingly important in accounting practice.

Adapted from ACCTG 322: Financial Reporting II, *University of Massachusetts Amherst, Ray Pfeiffer, Spring 2006.*

Example 4: Course Objectives
ABET Outcomes

The Department of Civil Engineering offers two ABET-accredited undergraduate degrees: Civil Engineering (CE) and Geological Engineering (GeoE). (*ABET* stands for Accreditation Board for Engineering and Technology.) To maintain ABET accreditation, the Department of Civil Engineering must demonstrate that all its graduates have the following eleven general skills and abilities. In this course, CE 4101 Project Management and Economics, the bolded outcomes will be specifically emphasized.

- **An ability to apply knowledge of mathematics, science, and engineering**

- An ability to design and conduct experiments, as well as to analyze and interpret data

- **An ability to design a system, component, or process to meet desired needs**

- **An ability to function on multidisciplinary teams**
- **An ability to identify, formulate, and solve engineering problems**
- **An understanding of professional and ethical responsibility**
- **An ability to communicate effectively**
- An ability to understand the impact of engineering solutions in a global and societal context
- A recognition of the need for, and an ability to engage in, lifelong learning
- **A knowledge of contemporary issues**
- **An ability to use the techniques, skills, and modern engineering tools necessary for engineering practice**

To successfully complete this course, you will be required to learn, develop, and ultimately demonstrate these skills and abilities within the context of this course.

Adapted from CE 4101W: Project Management and Economics, *University of Minnesota, Karl Smith and Randal Barnes, Fall 2002.*

Example 5: Course Objectives
Ability-Based Outcomes

1. Provide appropriate pharmacotherapy interventions to individual patients
   - Assist with access to health services

2. Maintain and enhance competence through self-initiated learning
   - Use regular self-assessment and peer assessment to identify learning needs and self-directed learning efforts
   - Identify and use resources to stay current and meet learning needs (e.g., professional libraries, pharmacy organizations, journals, and listservs)

3. Manage the pharmacy within the organization's business plan
   - Manage patients
   - Apply research and assessment methods to establish quality, values, and outcomes
   - Collaborate as an effective, efficient, and accountable team member

4. Develop practice and leadership

- Establish professional credibility
- Determine strengths, weaknesses, opportunities, and threats of the practice site
- Identify and prioritize changes needed to implement the ideal practice
- Create a plan of action to address needs
- Explore career pathways
- Develop and maintain a career plan

5. Participate in public health and professional initiatives and policies

- Contribute to government and public health initiatives and policy development
- Identify potential opportunities to serve the public and educate the public and other health professionals to improve health promotion and disease prevention
- Respond to disasters

6. Advance the profession

- Participate in professional organization activities
- Establish and maintain professional collaborations
- Evaluate own and peer's behavior against professional standards and take appropriate actions
- Advocate professional improvements

Applicable General Ability Outcomes

The relationship of the course objectives, instructional methods, and assessment methods to the programmatic outcomes is shown in the following:

1. Thinking abilities

- The student shall acquire, comprehend, apply, analyze, synthesize, and evaluate information.
- The student shall integrate these abilities to identify, resolve, and prevent problems and make appropriate decisions.

2. Communication abilities

- The student shall read, write, speak, listen, and use media to communicate.

3. Professional ethics and identity

- The student shall behave ethically.
- The student shall accept the responsibilities embodied in the principles of pharmaceutical care.

4. Social interaction, citizenship, and leadership

- The student shall demonstrate appropriate interpersonal and inter-group behaviors.

Adapted from PYPC 5210: Pharmacy Practice Development, Management and Evaluation I, *Auburn University, Salisa C. Westrick, Bill Felkey, and Jan Kavookjian, Fall 2006.*

Example 6: Course Objectives

I realize that most of you will not end up in jobs where your primary focus is on the mechanical behavior of materials. However, nearly every job requires *some* knowledge of how materials deform or break. Therefore, three to five years after taking this class, you should be able to:

1. Find out how to determine the mechanical properties of materials

    Use ASTM standards to find information about testing procedures. Interpret mechanical test results to obtain mechanical properties. Types of testing include tension, compression, fatigue, fracture, bending, hardness, creep, impact toughness, stress corrosion, crack growth, and nanoindentation.

2. Explain why different materials deform differently

    Use Hooke's law; find effective elastic moduli that result from constraint; explain anisotropic elasticity, plasticity, and dislocation motion. Determine slip systems and crystal structure. Compare ductile and brittle failure.

3. Calculate or predict the response of a material to an applied stress state

    Use tensors to describe stress/strain states. Calculate crack size and predict fracture stress. Use the generalized Hooke's law. Apply creep laws. Use yield criteria, models for plastic deformation, and deformation mechanism maps. Determine slip systems and crystal structure. Compare ductile and brittle failure.

4. Prescribe methods to improve the mechanical properties of materials

    Explain solid solution strengthening, precipitation hardening, dispersion strengthening, grain size refinement, transformation toughening, and formation of composite microstructures.

5. Decide whether a material is suitable for a given application.

Use deformation mechanism maps and yield criteria to predict behavior. Locate data on mechanical properties of materials. Explain trade-offs in mechanical properties.

Adapted from MSR 312: Mechanical Behavior of Materials, *Boise State University, Megan Frary, Spring 2007.*

Readings

Your syllabus will identify textbooks and readings for the course. Students will appreciate knowing where to find all the necessary materials. They will also appreciate knowing which materials are required, which you recommend they purchase, and which readings are relevant to upcoming topics and assignments. The selected readings can be included as part of the syllabus or can be produced as a separate course pack. Some libraries, such as the one at the University of Nevada, Reno, also allow you to put up electronic resources, such as out-of-print scanned book chapters, which you can reference in your syllabus. If readings are important to the course—and why would you assign them otherwise?—then it is a good idea to explain to students why you selected them and to provide guidelines for reading them. Obviously, if you plan to distribute copyrighted materials, you will need to obtain the necessary copyright clearances.

Example 1: Guide to the Readings

I want to take a moment to clarify how I hope you will approach the readings. The first rule is this: don't take the readings as gospel. Just because something is printed does not make it Absolute Truth. Be critical of what you are reading, drawing on your own experiences and other knowledge. I have chosen many readings precisely because they are provocative. If you find yourself strongly disagreeing with a particular reading, that's fine; indeed, I encourage strong disagreement. *However,* if you disagree, you must clarify in your mind the reasons and evidence on which you are basing your disagreement.

At the same time, keep an open mind. Listen to what the readings have to say. Think about other experiences you have had and reading you have done that might corroborate the course readings. Give yourself time to *reflect* on the information, insights, and perspectives offered in the readings. These are not readings to be run through rapidly. Take your time with them; allow yourself to enter into a kind of conversation with them.

Adapted from Eastern European History: From Independence to Independence, 1918 to the Present, *Syracuse University, Walter Ullmann and Jonathan P. G. Bach, 1993.*

Example 2: Readings for the Writing Studio

We put a good deal of effort into selecting the readings, and we believe the pieces we have here will help us accomplish the work of WRT 115 while at the same time provide intellectual stimulation and entertainment. Later in the course, we'll ask you how you feel about our choices.

Each of the course readings can work for you in at least two ways. They provide content—new knowledge or at least a new perspective on a topic with which you may already be familiar. Further, the readings serve as examples of the kinds of writing you yourself will be doing. For instance, in the first section of the course, where we ask you to write about your own reading and writing experiences, we provide essays in which the authors are going about the very same business. Later, in the third module, we ask you to observe some facets of life around you and to write about and interpret what you see. Then we supply chapters from books that work on that very project. Beyond that, all the readings are examples of different kinds of good writing, writing we hope you will savor, study, and choose at times to emulate. So look through the readings, see which writers you've heard of and which will constitute unexplored territory, sample sentences here and there, and whet your appetite. Then turn your attention back to this course guide and read the module descriptions.

Adapted from WRT 115: Writing Studio I: Course Guide, *Syracuse University, Nance Hahn, 1994.*

Example 3: Readings
Textbooks

Gumperz, J. J., & Levinson, S. C. (Eds.). (1996). *Rethinking Linguistic Relativity.* Cambridge: Cambridge University Press.

Whorf, B. L. (1956). *Language, Thought and Reality.* John B. Carroll (Ed.). Cambridge: MIT Press.

All the additional readings are available in two separate locations.

WebCT: The Ling 4100 WebCT page links to electronic files for downloading and/or printing.

Drawer: Or you can find a master photocopy of each of the readings in the Reading Drawer at the Linguistics Department office (Hellems 290). To make your personal photocopy, check out a master photocopy by listing your name, phone number, and time on the check-out sheet in the Ling 4100 file. Please return any master photocopies within the hour so that other students will also have access.

Adapted from Linguistics 4100: Perspectives on Language, *University of Colorado–Boulder, Les Sikos, 2006.*

Resources

The resource section is intended to guide students to course resources and encourage their use. Course resources can include published materials; individuals, including librarians and other faculty; writing, math, or media centers; and so forth. This section should list all materials that will be needed for the course as well as their location (e.g., the college bookstore, the reserve room at the library, the World Wide Web, your course management system, or a computer lab). If you are including a bibliography of publications relevant to course objectives and assignments, be sure to format it accurately using the style you require students to learn and use. If you are using a lab or resource room, be sure to tell the students where it is located, when it is open, and how they are to use it. Students may also need instructions for accessing resources on your course management system. If you are using personal response devises, commonly known as "clickers," be certain to indicate the model number and purchase details if your campus has not adopted a common model. You might also explain why books and other resources have been chosen and what their relative importance is to the course or discipline.

Example 1: Resources
Basic Statistics: Clinical and Health Related

Dawson, B., & Trapp, R. G. (2001). *Basic and clinical biostatistics* (3rd ed.). New York: McGraw-Hill.

Elston, R. C., & Johnson, W. D. (1987). *Essentials of biostatistics.* Philadelphia: F. A. Davis.

Glover, T., & Mitchell, K. (2002). An *introduction to biostatistics.* New York: McGraw-Hill.

Hassard, T. H. (1991). *Understanding biostatistics.* St. Louis, MO: Mosby.

Hirsch, R. P., & Riegelman, R. K. (1992). *Statistical first aid*: *Interpretation of health research data.* Boston: Blackwell Scientific.

Behavioral Science

Christensen, L. B., & Stoup, C. M. (1991). *Introduction to statistics for the social and behavioral sciences.* Pacific Grove, CA: Brooks/Cole.

Darlington, R. B., & Carlson, P. M. (1987). *Behavioral statistics: Logic and methods.* New York: Free Press.

Glass, G. V, & Hopkins, K. D. (1984). *Statistical methods in education and psychology* (2nd ed.). Englewood Cliffs, NJ: Prentice Hall.

Statistical Power Analysis

Murphy, K. R., & Myors, B. (2003). Statistical power analysis: A simple and general model for traditional and modern hypothesis tests (2nd ed.). Mahwah, NJ: Lawrence Erlbaum Associates.

Adapted from Nursing 110.501 Intermediate Biostatistics, *The Johns Hopkins University, Ron Berk, 2006.*

Example 2: Resources
Resources about Community or Cultural Contexts

"Word-work . . . is generative; it takes meaning that secures our difference, our human difference—the way in which we are like no other" (p. 22). T. Morrison, The Nobel Lecture in Literature, *1993*

Delpit, L. (1995). *Other people's children: Cultural conflict in the classroom.* New York: New Press. An educator's view of teachers as cultural brokers and how cultural clashes in the classroom impact the educational system.

Resources on Classroom Settings

"Be it grand or slender, burrowing or blasting or refusing to sanctify; whether it laughs out loud or is a cry without an alphabet, the choice word or chosen silence, unmolested language surges toward knowledge, not its destruction" (p. 21). T. Morrison, The Nobel Lecture in Literature, *1993*

Conroy, P. (1972). *Water is wide.* Boston: Houghton Mifflin.

Fedullo, M. (1992). *Light of the feather: A teacher's journey into Native American Classrooms and culture.* New York: Doubleday. A non-Native American teacher speaks of his experiences teaching in Native American classrooms.

Adapted from EDF 500.02 (#7059): Cultural Foundations of Education, *Northern Arizona University, Linda Shadiow, Fall 2005.*

Example 3: Resources
Web and Software Resources

WebCT. This course will use WebCT for posting individual and group presentations and writing assignments, instructor materials, and other resources. The address of the WebCT site is http://webct.umn.edu.

CritPath for Windows. Available from Karl Smith or downloadable from http://www.ce.umn.edu/~smith.

WinExp. Windows-based expert system shell. Available from Karl Smith for in-class use. Bundled with A. M. Starfield, K. A. Smith, & A. Bleloch. (1991). *How to model it: Problem solving for the computer age.* Edina, MN: Interaction Book.

Microsoft Project or whatever project management software you're familiar with. I'll use CritPath to demonstrate principles and will show examples from Microsoft Project. MS Project 2002 is included with Wysocki.

Adapted from MOT 8221: Project and Knowledge Management, *University of Minnesota, Karl Smith, Spring 2007.*

Example 4: Resources

Writing Center: The Writing Center in LIB 308 offers free tutoring. While the tutors will not proofread papers for grammar and spelling errors, they will help students with a variety of issues related to composing essays, such as getting started, audience awareness, organization, development of ideas, etc. When going to the Writing Center, it is always a good plan to have questions in mind and know what you want to work on. The Writing Center also offers computer software to help with grammar. Students may bring work in at any time during the writing process. No appointment is necessary. Writing Center hours are 8 A.M.–8 P.M. Monday–Thursday, 8 A.M.–2 P.M. on Friday, 9 A.M.–3 P.M. on Saturday, and noon–4 P.M. on Sunday. For quick help with specific grammar questions, call the Grammar Hotline at 913-469-4413.

Other support services: The Academic Achievement Center (LIB 227) has courses to help you with reading speed and comprehension, spelling, and vocabulary. The Career Center can help you with job placement and goal setting. The Counseling Center will help you plan your academic career.

Adapted from Composition 121, *Johnson County Community College, Ellen Mohr, Fall 2006.*

Course Calendar

Students often turn first to the schedule that lists topics, assignments, projects, exams, and due dates. They want to know what will be happening and when. Probably the most difficult planning decisions concern the structuring of course material. Ask yourself:

- How much can students cover in a typical semester?
- How can I structure these responsibilities so that they can be met despite other demands on students' time?
- What points should I emphasize?
- What textbook material can I omit or condense?
- How can I promote online learning?

When planning assignments, it is helpful to think of them as a sequence of learning activities. Consider those things you expect students to learn or do on their own and what you will do to help them process the information during classroom time. Ideally, you should conclude this sequence with feedback about learning. You can provide feedback in the classroom or by your comments on out-of-class assignments and in-class written activities.

You can govern the amount of work you expect from students by a general expectation of two hours of outside work for each contact (classroom) hour. For the average course, this usually means ten hours of homework per week. Some classes may require students to invest more than ten hours; sometimes the workload will vary from week to week. Most instructors, particularly those teaching upper-division or graduate courses, include writing requirements so that students improve their communication skills and research techniques.

In preparing the course schedule, keep in mind that your students must often balance academics, work, and family obligations. These concerns should not lead you to reduce course expectations. Your assignment schedule, however, should be organized to allow students time to meet your expectations. Consider placing heavy reading requirements or assignment due dates at the beginning of the week, giving students weekends to complete assignments. To help students organize their time, your syllabus could also reflect a step-by-step approach to major assignments. For a research paper that counts significantly toward the final grade, you can assign due dates for a working bibliography, an outline, and a rough draft. Be sure your schedule emphasizes, perhaps in bold type, the dates of exams and specific assignments. If possible, try to avoid scheduling major projects and exams during peak times when other instructors have also made heavy demands on students.

Your list of assignments should allow adjustments if your class should suddenly get involved in a spirited discussion that seems more worthwhile than a scheduled quiz or if you unexpectedly need to spend more time on a particular topic. Emphasize that the calendar is subject to revision depending on the needs of the class while reminding the students that they are also responsible for the material covered because of an adjustment. Students will also need to know how you will communicate the revised timetables or plans. It is a good idea to include key dates from the academic calendar (midterm, last day to drop a course without jeopardy, holidays) to maximize students' information about dates that may influence their planning decisions.

Example 1: Course Calendar
Class Schedule and Assignments

Date	Topics and Activities	Readings (due on this date)	Assignments (due on this date)
Theme One: My National and Cultural Identities			
Aug. 23	Course information Introduction: "Where I'm From?" poem Defining culture		Personal experience bag Personal information form Syllabus (read and comprehend)
Sept. 1	Cultural orientations Discuss the intercultural interview assignment	"American Values and Assumptions" by Gary Althen	Response paper based on survey and readings
Theme Two: American Practices, Norms, and Values			
Sept. 13	Intro: Stereotypes Our own multicultural identities Introduction to Jane Elliot's work	"The Social Cognition Approach to Stereotypes" by Margaret Matlin	Revision of cultural response paper due Submit questions for guest speakers
Sept. 15	Sunday morning: America's most segregated hour? Guest speakers: Barbara Brewton and John Comer, Presbyterian Church	*More Than Equals,* chapters 1 and 2	Interview questions due Written draft of stereotype paper on concepts chosen from Jane Elliot checklist

(Continued)

Date	Topics and Activities	Readings (due on this date)	Assignments (due on this date)
Theme Three: Others' Views of the United States			
Sept. 27	Discussion on "Walking Each Other Home" and multiethnic identities	Read international press about the United States (details forthcoming)	**Intercultural interview report due (15%)**
Oct. 4	Discussion of international press articles	Read international press about the United States	**Synthesis project plan due**

This is a tentative schedule. We'll give you as much advance notice as possible concerning any changes. The readings will be handouts, online, or on the Gumberg Library E-Reserves.

Adapted from CLPRG 430W Seminar on Intercultural Interpretations, *Duquesne University, Cynthia Lennox and Laurel Willingham-McLain, Fall 2005.*

Example 2: Course Calendar
Week 1: History of Evolutionary Biology

Objectives:

Identify major tenets of the Evolutionary Synthesis

Recognize the major breakthroughs of evolutionary thinking

Provide examples that supported Darwin's ideas

Reading: Chapters 1, 2, BB: *Origin of Species*, pp. 14–21

Lecture 1: Evolution before Darwin; Darwin's Contribution

Lecture 2: The Evolutionary Synthesis

Week 2: Variation and Its Sources

Objectives:

Define phenotype, genotype, locus, gene, allele, mutations, gene copy

Distinguish between sources of phenotypic variation

Determine principles of genetic variation in populations

Reading: Chapter 3

Lecture 3: Variation Principles

Lecture 4: Variation in Multiple Levels

Adapted from Biology 105: Evolution, *University of North Carolina at Chapel Hill, Tatiana Vasquez, 2006.*

Course Requirements

Include course requirements in your objectives and assignment schedule. Explicitly detail each requirement in a separate section of the syllabus or combine them with your grading policies. Many instructors prepare lengthy handouts during the term that elucidate the parameters of each requirement and guide students to attain each assignment's objectives. These should not replace a written explanation of the course requirements. Consider attaching extra material—explanations of the assigned case study, book review, paper, or class project, or helpful handouts with such titles as "Writing a Scientific Paper," "Guidelines for a Psychology Bullet Paper," or "Anatomy of a Book Review"—to the syllabus. The examples of course requirements were selected for inclusion in this section because they rely on process skills such as participation or teamwork to complete a requirement. Each offers insight into how learner-centered instructors are managing to focus on developing interpersonal skills as students master the course content.

Example 1: Class Participation

Discussing philosophical ideas is a great way to absorb a working knowledge of these ideas and to develop your own ideas in response to what is studied in class. Often you will find that your classmates have a different perspective and raise good questions about your ideas or add further insights to your ideas. You do have a lot to learn from each other—I know I find my own continued study enriched by hearing your ideas and perspectives, and so I am sure that you can learn as much from each other as I learn from all of you!

Class participation includes both venturing forth with your own ideas and questions and listening attentively to each other. A person who seldom speaks but listens intently and takes notes is participating as fully as one who speaks frequently and thoughtfully. In guiding discussion, I seldom impose the strict control required to ensure that everyone in class speaks equally because I respect the fact that different people have different preferences for how they participate in class discussion. I do impose the mild control of giving preference to new voices when I can tell that someone who has not spoken much wants to speak. And I very much encourage those who feel shy about speaking to *practice* speaking up because it is a liberation to find one's voice in discussion, and I will promise to do my best to try to keep the classroom a safe place to share ideas, even tentative, uncertain ideas! In the same spirit, I encourage those who find themselves speaking a lot to use their high level of social comfort well—you who speak a lot do much to shape the atmosphere of discussion, so work to make that atmosphere one that is warm and inviting. There are gentle ways that those who are vocal can try to make space and draw in those who are quiet. The quiet students appreciate when the confident vocal students take an interest in hearing their thoughts!

In discussions, *making connections*—with the readings, with topics discussed in previous classes, and with the comments that others have made in class—is especially helpful to you and to everyone else, and therefore is especially noted and appreciated.

Adapted from PHIL 204: Theories of Knowledge and Reality, *St. Lawrence University, Laura Rediehs, Fall 2006.*

Example 2: Class Participation

Each class member is expected to contribute to the dialogue/discussion. You may participate by:

1. Asking a question

2. Responding to a question asked by the moderator, faculty, guest presenter, or other class member

3. Making a comment or observation

It is important that you read the assigned papers as background information on the issue/topic before the seminar session. The abstract you prepare is to synthesize the main points from the readings and is not the place for you to present your personal opinions. The class discussion will provide you an opportunity to present your views and opinions on the topic for the week. *Your opinions and concerns are important, and you are encouraged to share them with the group.* Our goal is not to argue or to try to reach consensus of opinions on the issue but to share in dialogue with each person contributing. You are encouraged to listen carefully to what others have to say.

Be considerate of other class members at all times. Do not interrupt. There should be only one person speaking. Wait to be recognized by the moderator before speaking. The moderator is responsible for controlling and directing the dialogue. Do not start side conversations with another class member during the class. All contributions should be addressed to the whole class.

Each student should try to make at least one contribution to the dialogue each week. For some of you, this will be difficult because your natural inclination is to listen, not to speak. For others, you will need to restrain your desire to speak frequently. Some topics will be of greater interest to you than others, but your contribution is expected on a regular basis. Your participation will be monitored during each seminar, and your grade for class participation will be based on the contributions you make.

Adapted from RLEM 481: Current Issues in Range Management: Past, Present & Future, *Texas A&M University, M. M. Kothmann, Spring 2006.*

Example 3: Working in Groups
Newsletter Project

For this project, you will write and revise copy for a newsletter, edit and proofread the copy of other class members, and see a newsletter through the production process. You will be part of a group working on a specific newsletter. You will be evaluated as follows:

25% of final grade—the quality of the editing

> This includes both comprehensive editing and copyediting. Comprehensive issues include organization, format, and audience. Copyediting issues include consistency (use of effective style sheet), accuracy, style, completeness, visual effectiveness, correctness. An individual grade.

20% of final grade—the quality of the newsletter as a whole

> Considerations include overall appropriateness for audience and goals of publication; effective writing (well-developed, well-organized, interesting prose); visual and stylistic consistency; coherence without redundancy; clarity at sentence and word level. All members of the group receive the same grade for this part.

1. Writing Each group *member* must produce about a thousand words of original manuscript copy for a newsletter. *You can write one longer article or several shorter ones.* If you have four or five group members, your newsletter will be about four thousand to six thousand words total. Finished newsletters typically range from four to ten pages. Your copy must include at least some prose (in other words, lists of restaurants won't be sufficient). Possible types of articles include news stories, profiles, editors' columns, how-to pieces, etc. You are responsible for revising your writing several times during the semester.

2. Editing Editing takes place in two stages. In the first stage, you will do comprehensive editing of manuscripts submitted to your newsletter. This will consist of a letter to a writer detailing how he/she should revise the manuscripts. In addition, you will make comprehensive comments on the manuscript itself. In the second stage, you will copyedit the manuscript and develop a style sheet.

3. Production As a group of writers and editors for a newsletter, you will proofread copy, design a layout, cut as needed, develop headlines, create a newsletter style sheet, and publish a final newsletter. *This assignment is not graded on the graphic qualities of the newsletter (although it is wise to work on this if you wish to include the newsletter in future job portfolios).* I do expect you to produce a focused, well-written newsletter.

A note on group work: Most of the group work for this project will be done in class during times designated as "newsletter workshops." It is likely, however, that you will have to meet once or twice outside of scheduled class time.

At the end of the semester, you will distribute copies of the newsletter to all class members. Each of you should expect to spend up to $15.00 on copying costs for this project. Black-and-white copies are WAY cheaper than color copies. *You may want to print out a couple of color copies for show and the rest in black and white.*

WARNING: ALWAYS BACK UP COPIES OF YOUR NEWSLETTER ON DISKS OR ON THE L-DRIVE. I HAVE HEARD TOO MANY STORIES OF CRASHING H-DRIVES!

4. Roles of Group Members At the beginning of the project, you should divide up specialized tasks that are required in addition to the basic writing and editing. Here are the roles I would suggest for a group of four. You can juggle this if you have three or five members.

1. *Managing editor.* This person is responsible for making sure that group members submit copy on time, that the production schedule is followed, and that particular tasks are assigned as needed. The managing editor should keep a log of incoming and outgoing work. Pick someone who is organized and is willing to nag.

2. *Graphic artist.* This person should be responsible for the final layout of the newsletter. This doesn't mean that this person will be the only one doing the graphics, but he/she takes responsibility for getting it done. This person should have knowledge of a desktop publishing program like Publisher, InDesign, or Quark, or be willing to learn such a program during the semester.

3. *Utility writer.* This person writes filler as needed. If the newsletter is short, or if there's missing copy, this person writes so that there's the right amount of content. This person could also be responsible for suggesting cuts when needed and for writing effective headlines. This person should be a quick researcher and solid writer.

4. *Copy/production editor.* This person is responsible for getting the final copy proofread and duplicated in a timely and efficient fashion. This person should have excellent copyediting and proofing skills. He/she should also have a car and be punctual!

5. Option You may produce your newsletter as an online publication.

Adapted from WRIT 371: Editing, *Metropolitan State University, Anne Aronson, Spring 2005.*

Example 4: Working in Groups

Below are five premises that all class members should agree to in order to make the groups work effectively.

1. None of us is as smart as all of us.

   We need each other to complete this task well. Our job is to get all involved in our talk and in our various tasks. Some of us do some things better, but each of us does some things well. Everyone has resources to offer. We will share our wealth.

2. There are different ways to be a successful group.

   There is no one way to be a good group. Groups approach tasks differently. Groups work differently. There are lots of ways for us to meet the criteria for a good product. The style of our group does not dictate the substance. An orderly group is not always a productive one.

3. Process.

   We will check in with each other as we go. Let's ask our members regularly, "Are things going OK? What should we change to be a better group?" We will try to test and retest the soundness of our ideas and to test how much we agree. We will ask before moving on, "Are we making the right move here? Does everyone agree?" Although consensus will be one of our goals, we know it is not always realistic.

4. We intend to build a rewarding group experience.

   We will be grateful to our members for contributing. We hope to have a good group experience and intend to express our appreciation often to contributors and to ourselves when we show good group effort. We will give out "honorable mentions" to each other. We will try to use good judgment and tact in sharing our viewpoints and in responding to others' views. We will give feedback well.

5. We will not report to the instructor a group or individual problem that hasn't been discussed first in the group with all members present.

   We understand that there is no such thing as problem individuals; it's our group problem. We intend to handle personnel problems early and often. We will first attempt our own intervention before we approach an outside person.

Anything else?

One more thing: I expect all groups to function smoothly. If, under extraordinary circumstances, there is a severe problem in a group, I reserve the right to (a) make an alternate grading arrangement for the newsletter or (b) split the group up and assign alternate projects. This is an absolute last resort. (Adapted from materials by Suzanne Walfoort.)

Adapted from WRIT 371: Editing, *Metropolitan State University, Anne Aronson, Spring 2005.*

Example 5: Group Work in Problem-Based Learning
Guidelines: Why Do This?

Ethical problems do not occur in a vacuum; they occur in the context of clinical practice, with multiple members of the health care team, in families, and in society. They are messy real-life problems that health professionals deal with every day. Problem-based learning assumes that learning is KNOWING, UNDERSTANDING the perspective of others, and DOING. Active learning occurs through having students engaged and responsible for their learning. Some of the key features of problem-based learning are:

1. Problem-centered

2. Student-led teams

3. Emphasis on collaboration and analysis

4. Instructor is unobtrusive guide on the side

5. Emphasis on lifelong learning skills, problem-solving skills, and meeting-management skills

What Are We Going to Do?

Ethics Committee Consultation A large part of your small-group work will be done with your group acting as an ethics committee that is providing consultation to the individual who referred the case. We are going to implement a model of small-group discussion that has been used in the medical school as part of its problem-based curriculum. Many of these ideas come from Dr. Jos Welie's course materials and his article in *Medicine, Health Care, and Philosophy* (1999, volume 2, pages 195–203).

Students will work in their learning teams, and these groups will work together all semester. You will each have the responsibility to facilitate the small-group discussion as you and your partners will "chair" the ethics committee. You will also have the opportunity to write a counter case letter. Counter cases are descriptions of the same case from another person's perspective. The typical case will be written from the perspective of the physical therapist. Then the counter cases could be written from other perspectives, such as the patient and/or family members, nurse, MD, social worker, patient's lawyer, institution's risk management office, etc.

Adapted from PTD 435: Ethics in Physical Therapy Practice, *Creighton University, Gail Jensen, Spring 2006.*

Policies and Expectations: Attendance, Late Papers, Missed Tests, Class Behaviors, and Civility

Course policies are, of course, related to many other course components, such as your teaching philosophy, your expectations, and evaluation. Whether you make expectations or policies a separate section of the syllabus or simply fold them under other headings is entirely up to you. The critical decision is how to address issues—in a logical and straightforward way—that may negatively impact the course or students' behaviors. Whatever your pet peeves may be—cell phone calls, text messaging, Net surfing during class—try to avoid a scolding tone.

We recommend that you maintain attendance records. You may or may not decide to count attendance or class participation toward the final grade. Ideally, every class session should be so important that students will be eager to attend. Because some of your students will miss classes—because of athletic, academic, religious, or family obligations or because of illness—clarify your policies in writing.

Your attendance, participation, and make-up policies must be flexible but not overly permissive. If you count class participation toward the final term grade, be sure that you define this elusive phenomenon and emphasize its significance for the students. If online class participation is a requirement, is communicating in grammatically correct English expected? Are you looking for the number of times students speak up or for the quality of their commentary? If it's the latter, how will you determine the weight of a particular contribution? Will you let students know during the term how they are doing? Will active class participation substantively affect the final grade, or will you consider this only in borderline cases? Will lack of participation—especially by shy or insecure students or by those from cultures that encourage passive respect—adversely affect the final grade? How will confidentiality of information disclosed in a counseling practicum or a clinical internship be protected?

Keep those points in mind as you review the following examples.

Example 1: Attendance Policy

I will send around an attendance sheet each day at the beginning of class. You are responsible for making sure you sign the attendance sheet each day. You may miss one class without penalty. Beginning with your second absence, you will lose one percentage point from your final cumulative grade. *Save your absence for a legitimate emergency.* If you are absent, I assume you have a good reason for being gone. Therefore, I do not need doctors' notes or other documentation letting me know why you were absent. If a major emergency arises, let me know. Excessive absences—three or more—will result in failure of the course.

If you are absent from class, you are still responsible for the work assigned for that day, as well as any information given out that day. Please attempt to contact fellow classmates to find out what you missed before contacting me. Essays will be deducted one letter grade for each day they are late. Late daily assignments will receive only half credit but must be completed nevertheless.

Adapted from English 207: Introduction to Film Studies, *Frostburg University, Kevin Kehrwald, Fall 2006.*

Example 2: Attendance and Class Make-Up Policy

Regular on-time attendance in this course is expected. There is much that happens during class time that adds to your educational experience beyond what you can learn from just reading and writing in solitude. To come to college is to join a community of learners. An athlete who does not attend practices risks losing his or her place on the team. A musician or actor who does not attend rehearsals is usually not allowed to participate in the performance. So, too, is it questionable whether students who develop a habit of missing classes are really part of the class and deserve course credit.

Here, then, is the attendance policy for this course: you must make up each class that you miss by looking up (on *ANGEL*) the minutes a classmate has written on what happened in class on the day that you missed and by writing a two- to three-page response to the ideas discussed or presented in class that day. This response is due at the beginning of class when you return, to be sure that you are all caught up and prepared for that class session. It does not matter what the reasons are for missing class because it is a basic truth built into the space-time fabric of the universe that to miss class for any reason is to miss important material being covered, and it is your responsibility to show that you have indeed caught up on what you missed. If you miss more than two classes, you should meet with me (preferably during office hours) to explain what is going on.

Adapted from PHIL 204: Theories of Knowledge and Reality, *St. Lawrence University, Laura Rediehs, Fall 2006.*

Example 3: Expectations for Professional Behaviors

Students will treat their classroom obligations as they would treat any serious professional engagement. These obligations include:

1. Preparing thoroughly for each session in accordance with the course calendar and instructor's request

2. Adhering to deadlines and timetables established by the instructor

3. Participating fully and constructively in all course activities and discussions as scheduled

4. Displaying appropriate courtesy to all involved in the class sessions (courteous behavior specifically entails communicating in a manner that respects, and is sensitive to, the cultural, religious, sexual, and other individual differences in the SLU community)

5. Providing constructive feedback to faculty members regarding their performance

Adapted from BIOL 236-6L: Contemporary Issues in Biology, *Saint Louis University, Robert Grant, 2006.*

Example 4: Expectations for Rational and Intellectual Discussion

The basic assumption of this course is that learning results from a continuing process of rational discourse. Within the course, there are both opportunities and responsibilities. In this course, you have the opportunity to learn. Your responsibilities are to maximize your learning from the course (i.e., improve your intellectual understanding), to maximize and assist in the learning of your classmates, and to apply what you learn to your work. To take advantage of the opportunity and to meet your responsibilities, you are to:

1. Master the basic concepts, theories, methods, and heuristics. You are expected to know a great deal more after taking this course than you did before.

2. Think critically about the course content and topics to gain understanding and insights.

3. Explain precisely to several classmates your learnings, insights, and conclusions. Your learning is not complete until you teach what you know to someone else and can describe precisely what you have learned and what you understand.

4. Ask others to share their knowledge, conclusions, and insights with you. When they do so, listen carefully, elaborate by explaining how what you learned from them fits in with previous knowledge you have learned, and thank them.

5. Engage in intellectual controversy by taking positions counter to those of your classmates, developing clear rationales for your positions, challenging their reasoning and conclusions, and arguing the issues until you or they are logically persuaded.

Adapted from CE 4101W: Project Management and Economics, *University of Minnesota, Karl Smith and Randal Barnes, Fall 2002.*

Example 5: Expectations for Civil Behaviors

Any form of harassment against other students—including racist, sexist, homophobic, or threatening comments and behaviors—that creates a hostile environment will not be tolerated and is a violation of university harassment guidelines. It is also a violation of decent human behavior. Let's strive to create a classroom where respect for all people and diversity of opinion is the standard and desired. If you encounter a problem with civility and respect, please do not hesitate to come forward and talk to your instructor about it. We will find a means to address it and rectify it. You may also contact the student conduct code officer at 651–793–1540.

Unwelcome and unacceptable student behaviors:

Sleeping or daydreaming during class.

Chronic tardiness. Be here when class starts!

Reading or working on materials that are extraneous to the course.

Prematurely packing up your books and bags before class has ended.

Chatting with your classmates during a lecture or when classmates are delivering speeches.

Checking your cell phones or other electronic devices. All cell phones must be turned off.

Adapted from COMM 103: Public Speaking, *Metropolitan State University, Lori Schroeder, Fall 2006.*

Example 6: Expectations and Responsibilities
Class ground rules

This class involves participation in discussions and activities. We each have different experiences that influence our perspectives of the world. You may feel uncomfortable or disagree with certain ideas or opinions expressed by others or with certain topics in this class. You may also find you share perspectives or experiences with others. The classroom should be a lively, interactive, and comfortable place where information is shared, ideas tested, and issues debated.

We (students, TAs, and instructors) will strive to create an open, respectful, and trusting environment in this course. At minimum, the following rules will be practiced:

- **Cell phones and pagers will be turned off before entering the classroom.** If you answer a phone or pager during class, you will be asked to leave and will be marked absent for that day.

- Drinks in class are okay, but not food—you may not eat your lunch during class.

- Take care of any physiological needs *before* coming into the classroom.

- Everyone in class has both a right and an obligation to participate in discussions, and, if called upon, should try to respond.

- All questions, perspectives, and opinions are important and valuable—you are encouraged to share and discuss.

- Demonstrate respect for ideas, beliefs, and people.

- Avoid making assumptions, generalizations, or stereotypes.

- Recognize that opinions are just that.

- Always listen carefully, with an open mind, to the contributions of others.

- Ask for clarification when you don't understand a point someone has made.

- If you are offended or hurt by our or another's remarks, please let us know (anonymously if you prefer by dropping a note or telling a teaching assistant). We will make every attempt to effectively address the issue for all involved.

- Be able to use WebCT to participate in the class (look for documents and files, check grades, take quizzes, etc.). You are responsible for learning how to navigate in WebCT—if you don't know how, use the tutorials or go to the Help Desk at Getchell. There will be a brief overview the first week of class, but you must use it and click around on it to become literate on it.

- No missing classes for dental, doctor, or any personal appointments. These are considered unexcused absences.

- You will be assigned to learning groups within the first few weeks of class. You will remain with that group all semester.

- All assignments are to be turned in to your learning group folder in class. All assignments will be returned in the same folder. The learning group folders will be picked up before class begins by the week's group leader.

Student responsibilities

- Read, sign, and submit the Memorandum of Understanding.

- Submit all assignments complete, according to instructions, and on time—no late assignments.

- Attend and be prepared for class by reading and completing all assigned work in advance.

- Actively participate in lectures, discussions, and activities.

- Provide and consider constructive evaluations and feedback.

- Cooperate with, support, and be respectful of your colleagues and the instructor.

- Communicate with faculty or TA concerning any issue or difficulty, preferably *before* it becomes a significant problem.

- Make a full effort on all assignments—do not pick for points. I will do all I can to be fair, but you earn your grades.

- Adhere to the university's academic standards including those governing academic dishonesty, including cheating, plagiarism (submitting the language, ideas, thoughts or work of another as one's own, or allowing another to use your work in this way), or fraud. All exams are to be taken without the aid of books, notes, study sheets, other persons, any electronic device (such as cell phones, PDAs, Blackberrys, computers), or any other method. Serious grading consequences will result for students accused of academic dishonesty and will follow established university and School of Public Health policy. If you have any questions regarding what constitutes plagiarism, talk with me or consult the APA style manual.

- Demonstrate ethical behavior.

Faculty Responsibilities

- Provide course content that is timely, pertinent, and current based on sound research, not hearsay.

- Be on time and prepared for all classes.

- Provide consultation, advisement, and/or problem-solving time for students.

- Provide clear instructions regarding assignments and expectations.

- Be prepared to provide and consider feedback.

- Honor and respect students.

- Demonstrate ethical behavior.

- Provide and consider constructive evaluations and feedback.

- Return assignments in a timely manner (usually within one week, with the exception of the personal assessment).

Memorandum of Understanding: HE 201

I, _____ have read the course syllabus for HE 201 and understand the contents.

I have been given the opportunity to ask for clarification on any questions I had about the assignments, the exams, or any of the expectations of this course.

I am satisfied that my questions have been answered.

I agree to abide by the standards and expectations as stated, which includes ethical standards.

I agree to abide by the definition of and the procedure for academic dishonesty as defined by the University of Nevada, Reno, catalog.

Signed: _____

Date: _____

This memorandum of understanding must be signed and returned to the instructor no later than September 10, 2007.

Adapted from HE 201: Foundations of Personal Health and Wellness, *University of Nevada-Reno, Nora Constantino and Melanie Minarik, Fall 2007.*

Example 7: Expectations for Classroom Conduct

During our course, we will discuss many issues that are relevant to the ethical behavior of criminal justice system professionals. Some issues may be controversial and may lead to disagreements of opinion and personal beliefs. It is important that these differences be discussed and addressed and that these exchanges are conducted in an environment that affords mutual respect and dignity for all students. Intelligent people can and will disagree about these issues. In our discussions, it is expected that one person will speak at a time and that all students will have an opportunity to engage in these discussions, free from harassment, intimidation, or other expressions meant to discourage or disparage their participation. The instructors will confront and eliminate language or actions that are demeaning or offensive to others and, if not corrected, will exclude offenders from classroom participation.

Adapted from CJS 375: Criminal Justice Ethics, *Metropolitan State University, Mark Matthews and John Delmonico, Spring 2007.*

Example 8: Participation and Civility

Active participation is *required*. Because this is a seminar, *each one of us is responsible for contributing to the learning that takes place in class.* Participation in class means both sharing your ideas (by talking) *and* respecting and engaging the ideas of your classmates (by actively listening and responding). I keep track of all class participation.

I like what Bill Rose, a government professor here at the college, writes about the importance of civil discussion:

> *Respectful discussion, debate, and inquiry are at the heart of the academic enterprise. Advocating civility does not symbolize a retreat from passionate argument. On the contrary, it acknowledges that meaningful and constructive dialogue requires a certain degree of mutual respect, willingness to listen, and tolerance for opposing points of view. Classroom and on-line discussions, like any academic discourse, should follow norms of decency and effective communication. Debates should attack ideas but never the individuals who hold opposing views. A civil atmosphere, moreover, contributes to the objective assessment of various ideas, with attention to the strength of evidence presented and to alternative explanations. Classes that establish norms for respectful dialogue and reasoned debate can empower students to argue constructively and convincingly, to grow through rigorous intellectual exchange, and to prepare them for life in a complex, pluralistic world.*

We will discuss guidelines for classroom participation and discussion at the beginning of the semester.

As part of class participation, throughout the semester there will also be a variety of ungraded in-class writing assignments that count as participation.

Adapted from First-Year Seminar 105: England and the End of Empire: Recent English Fiction and Culture, 1980–Present, *Connecticut College, Michael Reder, Fall 2006. William Rose developed the paragraph on civil discussion for the government courses that he teaches at Connecticut College. Copyright 2006, Michael Reder.*

Example 9: Expectations and Preparation for Course Success

Psychology is a complex field with relevance and applications to all disciplines. My goal is to make EdPsych 312 interesting and informative by structuring the semester to actively engage you in learning. Content becomes meaningful as you apply 312 concepts to what you already know, to yourself as a learner, and to yourself as a developing teacher. EdPsych 312 activities and assignments are designed to support you as you acquire the knowledge base to apply, analyze, and evaluate teaching and learning processes. These are the tools a responsible teacher needs.

In EdPsych 312, you'll learn that effective learning is active. One challenge is to abandon an understanding of learning as receiving knowledge. What you'll experience this semester will generalize to classes you will be teaching. Welcome.

As the semester begins, we'll identify and acquire the skills needed to work productively in small groups. Anticipate this now: the case study and various in-class activities will require groups of at least four or five people. Field experiences will be done in pairs and require observations in public school settings. Begin now to work this into your personal schedules. Begin by pairing with a future teacher whose professional goals complement yours. When choosing partners, give consideration to class schedules, home proximity, and personal compatibility.

It is important to have a successful experience in EdPsych 312. Class participation and attendance is essential for success. Adopting a professional attitude about learning and about the knowledge you are acquiring is equally important. For these reasons, keep me informed when illness or personal demands interfere with your work. Just as a teacher calls in sick and makes arrangements for an absence from school, please contact me before you miss a class. Clarify assignments with classmates or me rather than coming to class unprepared. Please use the syllabus to pace your reading of the text and assignments. Knowledge cumulates. Requirements are due in a specific order. Respecting the due dates keeps you focused and on schedule. This is important because delayed grades will not be assigned. Requests for exceptions to these policies are best discussed in advance. Adherence to the Student Conduct Code of the university is expected.

Adapted from EDPSY 312, Psychology of Teaching and Learning, *University of Missouri–St. Louis, Margaret W. Cohen, Spring 2000.*

Example 10: Expectations for Using Wireless Technologies in Class

Feel free to bring your laptops or other technology tools that you use to take notes or manage your information, but use them respectfully. Respect your instructor and your fellow students by:

- Turning your cell phones or other potentially noise-making gadgets to silent or vibrate. Like a friendly flight attendant, I will remind you to do this at the beginning of every class.

- Leaving the classroom to take important calls rather than carrying on a conversation in class.

- Refraining from surfing the Web and chatting on your laptops during class. You may think you are being subtle but chances are that other people are noticing and are being distracted.

- Not talking among yourselves when the instructor or a fellow student is addressing the class.

Though failure to follow these guidelines will not affect your grade, it is unprofessional and will not gain you any esteem in the eyes of the instructor or your fellow students, who are your future colleagues.

Adapted from INLS 151: Organization of Information in a Digital Environment, *University of North Carolina at Chapel Hill, Kristina M. Spurgin, Spring 2004.*

Policies and Expectations: Academic Integrity, Disability Access, and Safety

Campus policies and expectations differ (in a legal sense) from the informal course expectations and policies offered in the previous section. Campuswide policies are the formal statements that convey the university's or college's legal rules and regulations. It is a good idea to refer to these legal rules and regulations in your syllabus for two reasons. First, referencing the policies indicates that you are invoking the authority of the regulatory boards of the campus to justify the behavioral norms for your course. That's a powerful statement. Second, you convey that you value lifelong learning by educating those in your classes about the standards of your profession and the state and federal policies that drive programmatic and institutional policies and procedures. Let students know how important these policies are to the campus community by pointing students to the formal statements in campus publications and on the campus's Web pages.

It is reasonable to predict that there will be an increase in the number of campuses that mandate including standardized statements of certain institutional policies in course syllabi. This is a result of concerns about how a campus prepares its faculty and staff to manage crisis situations. Whether a situation is a result of the actions of a troubled individual or an unintentional mistake by a lab assistant working with hazardous materials, every campus citizen must know where to turn immediately for alerts and assistance. Now that syllabi are available online and in course management systems, they can readily be linked to actual policies on a campus's Web pages.

Example 1: Academic Honesty

While the design of the course assignments and products associated with this course decreases concerns about plagiarism and academic dishonesty, it is important to acknowledge that, consistent with Monmouth University policy, "students caught plagiarizing papers and written work and/or cheating on examinations will receive an automatic F for the class and will be referred to the Associate Vice President for Administration for further disciplinary action."

Recognizing that plagiarism can also be the result of inadequate knowledge regarding how to construct papers that adequately reference others' work, students are invited to visit the following Web sites. These sites do a wonderful job of clarifying what constitutes plagiarism, providing examples and/or online tests of understanding: http://www.princeton.edu/pr/pub/integrity/pages/plagiarism.html and http://education.indiana.edu/~frick/plagiarism/.

Adapted from PR 498-50: Community Development across the Globe, *Monmouth University, Bonnie Mullinix, Fall 2003.*

Example 2: Academic Honesty

Academics with Honor. For this assignment, you may work with anyone. You must acknowledge all help received, in a detailed and descriptive way, on an acknowledgments page attached after your works cited page.

Adapted from English 211: Literature and Intermediate Composition, *United States Air Force Academy, Barbara Millis, Spring 2002. Section cited was developed by Tom Krise, former course director at the United States Air Force Academy and now professor of English at University of Central Florida.*

Example 3: Academic Honesty

Columbia College is a community of scholars that considers academic integrity essential to its sustenance. Since cheating, which includes plagiarism in all its forms, is prohibited both by the Honor Code and the Student Code of Conduct, *students guilty of plagiarism and/or other forms of cheating will fail the course and be brought before the Academic Honor Council for further sanctions.*

The first resource you should check on academic integrity is the college's very useful "Writing in the Disciplines" Web site: http://www.columbiacollegesc.edu/WID. It contains valuable links to "Defining and Avoiding Plagiarism," "Using Sources Effectively," and "Documentation Styles"—everything you need to know about using sources ethically and wisely, including citation styles used in various disciplines and actual models of successful research papers.

In English 101 (and perhaps in other courses), students cover citation issues usually in the first weeks of the class, using the *Harbrace College Handbook* and *Using Sources Effectively* as guides to proper documentation before writing assignments. From that point on, you are responsible for knowing and abiding by such guidelines for honest, effective research and writing. If you are unsure of the rules and you are an English 101 student who has completed the first part of the course, or you are a student enrolled in any course after English 101 that requires writing, you are responsible for conferring with the professor on your own to learn what you do not know. After you submit an assignment, you are subject to the rules of the Honor Code and its sanctions. If you are a transfer student who has not taken English 101 at Columbia College or who has placed out of it, you are still responsible for the material covered on academic integrity.

Academic dishonesty includes the following offenses:

- Claiming as your own work a paper written by another student.

- Turning in a paper that is largely a restatement in your own words of a paper written by someone else, *even if you give credit to that person for those ideas.* The thesis and organizing principles of a paper must be your own.

- Turning in a paper that contains paraphrases of someone else's ideas but does not give proper credit to that person for those ideas.

- Turning in a paper that uses the exact words of another author without using quotation marks, *even if proper credit is given in a parenthetical citation*, or that changes the words only slightly and claims them to be paraphrases.

- Turning in the same paper, *even in a different version,* for two different courses without the permission of *both* professors involved.

Web sites for useful student information on plagiarism:

http://www.princeton.edu/pr/pub/integrity

http://albany.edu/cetl/teaching/plagiarism.html

http://www.northwestern.edu/uacc/plagiar.html

http://sja.ucdavis.edu/avoid.htm

http://online.fsu.edu/learningresources/plagiarism/student.html

http://library.msstate.edu/li/tutorial/plagiarism

Do you really understand *plagiarism* and why it is such an offense to an academic community? Try this self-assessment tool to test your real knowledge: http://education.indiana.edu/~frick/plagiarism/.

And just in case you're curious about the depth of faculty knowledge of academic integrity and issues of plagiarism and how to detect and deal with academic dishonesty, take a look at this site, a brief glimpse at shared faculty interest in the topic: http://www.academicintegrity.org.

Columbia College is a member of the organization, and faculty are very knowledgeable of the myriad ways in which students get into trouble through plagiarism of print and Web sources.

Also, be aware that the insidious plethora of Web sites that offer plagiarized papers online can seduce you into a severe offense, especially when you've procrastinated and you're feeling undue pressure from deadlines. Papers downloaded from such sites are easily discovered by faculty with available tools such as http://www.turnitin.com, http://www.plagiarism.com, http://www.canexus.com/eve, http://www.google.com, and other powerful detection software.

Please remember that *honor* is part of what *honors* is all about!

Adapted from English 310 N (Honors): The Psychological Novel, *Columbia College, John Zubizarreta, Fall 2006.*

Example 4: Disabilities Statement

The Americans with Disabilities Act is a federal antidiscrimination statute that provides comprehensive civil rights protection for persons with disabilities. Among other things, this legislation requires that all students with disabilities be guaranteed a learning environment that provides for reasonable accommodation of their disabilities. Any student with a disability who needs academic adjustments or accommodations should approach the instructor and the Department of Student Life's Services for Students with Disabilities (in Room 126 of the Koldus Building) or call 979-845-1637. All discussions will remain confidential.

Adapted from MEEN 357: Engineering Analysis for Mechanical Engineers, *Texas A&M University, Raymundo Arróyave, Spring 2007.*

Example 5: Disabilities Statement

Students with special needs as addressed by the Americans with Disabilities Act who need assistance should contact Disability Access Services, 144 MSC (314-516-6554) immediately. Please meet with me early in the semester if you require accommodations. I will make reasonable efforts to accommodate your special needs.

The UMSL 2006–2007 Student Planner includes information on university and campus policies and procedures that provide the framework for working, teaching, and learning at UMSL. This information is also available online at http://www.umsl.edu/services/disabled/. I respect and adhere to these policies. Please be aware of and consult these policies and the planner for information about classroom accommodations, confidentiality, nondiscrimination, positive work environments, technology use, and student conduct.

Adapted from EDPSY 7647: Teaching for Learning in the University, *University of Missouri–St. Louis, Margaret W. Cohen, Fall 2006.*

Example 6: Safety

Students entering physical science classes should be aware that they may be in close contact with potentially hazardous chemicals and equipment. The students should assume responsibility for conducting themselves in a manner to minimize such hazards. *It is in the best interest of students who are pregnant to defer laboratory classes until after delivery.* Chemical hazards dictate that goggles, shoes, and protective covering will be worn whenever chemicals are used in the laboratory. Consumption of food, beverages, or tobacco is strictly prohibited and will not be tolerated. Unauthorized experiments are prohibited.

Adapted from CHEM 122: Principles of Chemistry, *Johnson County Community College, Kevin Gratton and Csilla Duneczky, 2005.*

Example 7: Campus Crisis Preparedness

New Mexico Junior College is committed to providing a safe environment for all visitors, staff, and students. This emergency/critical incident information sheet is intended to highlight potential areas of risk to campus personnel and facilities. New Mexico Junior College has identified potential risks and has prepared a plan for emergencies. This will not prepare you for all eventualities but is intended to give the student a basic awareness of disaster preparedness. Please familiarize yourself with the information provided and be prepared to take action in the event of an emergency. (Students are encouraged to notify faculty of potential medical conditions that may require emergency response.)

From Interpersonal Communication Syllabus, *New Mexico Junior College. Retrieved July 11, 2007, from http://www.nmjc.edu/asp-prod/webview/syllabi.asp? courseid=SE113&section=25014.*

Example 8: Campus Safety

The campus contracts with off-duty members of the West Plains Police Department, the Howell County Sheriff's Department, and/or certified individuals to provide the Evening Safety Services program. These services include a campus security presence, escort service, and emergency services. In the event of an evening emergency, please call the Garnett Library (417-255-7945) or the Evening Safety personnel (417-257-9078). See the emergency procedures for fire, tornado, and general campus assistance posted in the classroom. Additional information regarding campus safety may be accessed at http://www.wp.MissouriState.Edu/CampusSafety.

From Master Syllabus, Missouri State University. *Retrieved July 11, 2007, from http://www.wp.missouristate.edu/Academics/3388.htm*

Evaluation

As well as being told about the purpose of course requirements, students should know how their progress will be assessed, how their work will be evaluated, how grades will be assigned, and how those grades contribute to their final course grade. Your syllabus should include clear standards and criteria for any assessment strategies you will use. That information provides direction and focuses students on the goals of each activity. Evaluation or assessment is a great deal more than giving a grade. The major part of evaluation, whether during the course or as a final summary of achievement, should be in the form of comments on projects and papers, responses to student presentations, conversations, and other means of helping students understand how they can do better.

Evaluation can be done by both instructors and students. If peer review is built into your course, then you must address both the logistics and the ethics involved. Evaluation should include ongoing assessment procedures that allow students to learn to assess their own level of knowledge or skills. Many researchers are now emphasizing the importance of metacognition—having students think about their learning and assess their own progress. Bransford, Brown, and Cocking (2002), for example, identify metacognition as one of three key learning principles and exhort faculty to embed it within an integrated curriculum. Fink's (2003) new "Taxonomy of Significant Learning" includes a key component of "Learning How to Learn." Ongoing assessment helps students improve while the course or unit is under way, rather than only receiving feedback with an end-of-term evaluation. One way to offer a self-assessment is to ask students to compare their own essays, for example, to several examples from a previous term that have been annotated with ratings of inadequate, satisfactory, and excellent. When one of the purposes of your course is that students learn to evaluate their own work, explanations of self-evaluation procedures should be included in your syllabus. You and your students should know and rely on a variety of assessment procedures (Angelo & Cross, 1993). Your syllabus can provide materials that will clarify the process for your students.

If your students will be writing papers, developing media productions, conducting research, or developing portfolios, they need to know what constitutes successful completion. If students will be taking exams, they should know when the exams will be given, what material will be covered, what percentage of their final grade will be involved, if there will be a make-up exam, and what form the exam will take. Students usually want to know what types of questions will appear on a test (multiple choice, cases or problems, essays, etc.), as well as whether it is take home, in class, open book, or closed book.

Experimental activities—including various laboratory sessions, internships, and fieldwork placements—often involve different evaluation systems and personnel. It is important that both the student and the evaluator have a clear understanding of the criteria and methodology used.

Example 1: Essay

For your first writing assignment, I would like you to write a profile of a nearby place. Length is to be four or more double-spaced pages (not fewer than four full pages, not more than ten pages).

Please use this assignment sheet to guide your writing and development of a good first draft:

- Choose a place in the metropolitan area that's important to you; choose any place you like, though it will probably be easier if the place has significant natural elements.

- Describe it; appeal to our senses; use action verbs so the description is lively; don't bunch the description but place it where it is useful and pleasing.

- Go behind the scenes to gather information; use observation (visit the place, identify elements, and study what goes on), library and Web research, community resources, interviews with people nearby, and personal experience.

- Use the typical profile form or an adaptation of it:

    1. An opener that explains why the subject is interesting now

    2. A narrow, focused, and unifying theme

    3. An organizational scheme: present, recent past, deep past, future

    4. Description, facts, anecdotes, and quotes to support every paragraph

- Write with vigor and economy: use action verbs whenever possible.

- Create flow (unity) and coherence: unify paragraphs, write transitions between paragraphs, and use techniques for coherence, such as repetition of key terms.

- Write for a college-educated audience that enjoys play with language.

- Work with your awareness of place: if an emphasis on place is new to you, acknowledge it and work with it—for example, "the first time I've seen . . ."—and demonstrate your new awareness by capitalizing on ideas presented in class or in the reading.

- Work with and explain any filters or lenses through which you see nearby places: if you have lived elsewhere and see the Twin Cities through or in comparison to that previous place, then it may be useful to explain how you see local surroundings through such a lens.

- Discuss ambiguities, contradictions, or ironies that emerge during your reflection on your understanding of place (tension between old and new attitudes often makes for good writing).

- Discuss the nearby place in light of your awareness of ecology.

- Possibly discuss the nearby place in light of prose, poetry, or films that you enjoy.

- Use scenes—brief stories or anecdotes—to illustrate your ideas, insights, or attitudes about the nearby place, including how those ideas or attitudes are changing.

Adapted from WRIT 532: Writing about Place, *Metropolitan State University, Brian Nerney, 2006. Copyright 2006.*

Example 2: Peer Assessment

Peer reviews will be assessed for thoughtfulness, thoroughness, and your attention to clearly identifying problems and suggesting solutions. Of course, I want you to be kind and considerate as you offer your honest advice! You can (and should) balance suggestions for how to fix weak spots or how to address problems with sections that are primarily composed of "cheerleading" comments. BUT nobody in class is an expert presenter; therefore, if your peer review says, "Everything was just great . . . I loved how you . . . and I really liked how you . . . and when you . . . that was even better . . ." and offers no constructive advice, you will receive 50% of the possible points because you have only done half your job. *Substantive and important criticism* is a unique and thoughtful service that you can provide to your classmates and to others as you continue in your careers and lives outside St. Lawrence University; therefore, you should take this task seriously.

Adapted from PSYCH 317-A: Abnormal Psychology, *St. Lawrence University, Pamela Thacher, Fall 2006.*

Example 3: Self-Evaluation
Self-Evaluation of Sector Team Presentation

Presentation Team Topic: _____

Date: _____

Name: _____

Scoring Reference Key:

$0-1 = \, < 60\%$ (D)

$2-4 = 70-79\%$ (C)

$5-7 = 80-89\%$ (B)

$8-10 = 90-100\%$ (A)

A. Overall Group Presentation	35%
Our group was well prepared. Each member contributed equally in the preparation and had collected information from a variety of appropriate sources that were solid and relevant to the presentation of our topic. The session we facilitated was clear and creative and clearly built on our understanding of the sector as it impacts community development. We paced ourselves appropriately during the presentation and balanced time among and flow between our team members effectively. The presentation and activities followed a clear and logical sequence, and support materials were effectively and appropriately used. Our lesson presentation strategy was engaging and encouraged the active involvement of class members	10 9 8
Our group was fairly well prepared. We had all collected and critiqued cases. The session we facilitated was logically presented and built on our understanding of the sector as it impacts community development. We paced ourselves appropriately during the presentation and balanced time among and flow between our team members effectively. The presentation and activities was sequential, and support materials were appropriately used. Our session presentation strategy invited involvement from class members.	7 6 5
Our presentation was uneven and demonstrated that a few members had done most of the work. Although we shared information, most of it was collected by one or two of us and did not truly represent a group effort. The sources of information we did use were simply lesson plans that we collected. Our presentation consisted primarily of reading from notes and did little to engage participants in any meaningful way.	4 3 2

(Continued)

We did not prepare for this presentation as well as we should have. We did little to critique the lessons we gathered . . . All our information was available from the assigned readings in the text, and little, if any, outside reading was done in preparation. We did not have an engaging activity at all and basically read contributions in turn.	1 0

B. Critique and Discussion (In Class and Online)   25%

Our group was fully prepared for the questions asked during/after our presentation. We had in-depth knowledge of the sector we reviewed and were able to clearly articulate the issues and define the terms associated with our sector and describe how it impacts community development efforts. Through facilitation of the discussion, we were able to demonstrate our extended knowledge of the sector when answering specific questions. The answers to the questions asked provided a means to further illuminate the sector and the class's understanding of it.	10 9 8
Our group was able to answer some, but not all, of the questions completely. In our answers, we displayed our knowledge of the sector we reviewed and were able to identify the issues, define the terms associated with our sector, and describe how it impacts community development efforts. Through facilitation of the discussion, we were able to demonstrate our knowledge of the sector when answering specific questions. The answers to the questions asked provided a means to further illuminate the sector and the class's understanding of it.	7 6 5
The information we had collected, while sufficient to design and present our lesson, was insufficient to handle the questions asked by our peers. We were not sufficiently familiar with the sector to take the class clearly through the issues and define terms. Many of our answers consisted of restating the points we had made earlier.	4 3 2
We were unable to answer many/most of the questions put to us.	1 0

C. Supporting Documentation (Written Products)   25%

Our team submission and support materials (session plan, reference sheet, and handouts/Web postings) were complete, clearly communicated, and comprehensive and accurately matched our actual presentation and roles. The reference sheet was clear, well formatted, and well annotated and supplied a substantial number of references that covered the sector appropriately. Each member contributed equally in the preparation of the document.	10 9 8
Our team session plan, reference sheet, and support materials (handouts/Web postings) were complete, well communicated, and clear and generally reflected our presentation and designated roles. The reference sheet was clear, well formatted, and well annotated and supplied references that covered the sector. Each member contributed equally in the preparation of the document.	7 6 5
Our presentation session plan was somewhat unclear or not well communicated and did not include all components or did not reflect our presentation or individual roles. References were of poor or questionable quality, not annotated, or poorly formatted and/or were not relevant to the presentation or sector focus. Some members contributed substantially more to the document and its preparation than others, and there was only minimal effort made to produce a coordinated, coherent document.	4 3 2

Our presentation lesson plan was unclear and did not reflect our presentation. The written materials demonstrated our lack of coordination as a team. References were of poor or questionable quality and were not relevant to the presentation or topic. One person did all the work on the supporting documentation, which was not coherent.	1 0

D. Individual Self-Assessment (Personal Performance) — 15%

I feel my preparation was comprehensive and added greatly to our effort. My information matched the other information in the group well and was not redundant since we had coordinated our research efforts ahead of time. My contribution fit with the level of the rest of the group, which overall was very high.	10 9 8
My section of the presentation went well but was not coordinated as well as it could have been with the rest of the members of my group. While some of the information I shared was appropriate, I feel that some of the information I had brought to the presentation may not have been relevant. Overall, my contribution made sense and supported our team goal.	7 6 5
My contribution to the group effort appeared weak. I made some contributions to either the session or the discussion facilitation, but it did not seem to be at the level of other members or the standard I have seen in other groups' presentations. I relied mostly on the other group members to carry the presentation and read my contribution from notes.	4 3 2
I was not prepared for this presentation and read or presented information provided by my peers.	1 0

Adapted from PR 498-50: Community Development across the Globe, *Monmouth University, Bonnie Mullinix, Fall 2003.*

Example 4: Learning Contract

By the end of the semester each participant, in concert with the guidance of the instructor and other learners, will be responsible for systematic inquiry meant to deepen their commitment to lifelong learning, as follows:

1. Develop a personal learning contract consistent with the purpose and learning objectives of this course. It will conform to the format and guidelines proposed by Malcolm S. Knowles (see material saved online in Blackboard Course Documents folder > Learning Contract), including learning objectives, learning strategies and resources, evidence of accomplishment of objectives, and criteria and means for validating evidence, with estimated time involved and target dates for each objective.

2. Negotiate for the grade you are to receive for the course.

3. Develop an in-depth study of the philosophical foundations of adult education.

4. Learn all you possibly can about an area of the philosophies of adult education in which you are interested.

5. Be involved in engaging the other members of this class in an active learning experience of that area of interest.

Adapted from AduEd 6412: Philosophical Foundations of Adult Education, *University of Missouri–St. Louis, John Henschke and Pi-Chi Han, Fall 2007.*

Example 5: Portfolio

The concept of a portfolio is adapted from the artist's world. Each is individualized to best present you and your work for a particular purpose. The purpose influences what is included in the document. For EdPsych 7647, the portfolio is designed to present your semester's work and how you think about what you are learning.

This collection of materials (often referred to as "artifacts") is organized to show what you are able to do and, in the case of a course, what you have learned during the semester. It can document teaching preparation, classroom performance, professional growth, and evidence of reflective thinking of these activities. It is essential that each artifact is accompanied by a written rationale (reflection) explaining why it is included.

In the rationale, explain each entry for this course by assessing the effectiveness of the requirement for you as a learner. Indicate which course objectives it met, the ways that you use or plan to use the knowledge, and questions about the artifact that are unresolved or that you will seek in the future. In the future, you will have the task of adapting this all-inclusive portfolio into a teaching portfolio. Be concise as you write the rationale for each document; each should be about a paragraph long. Limit the total number of pages for the rationales to six pages. There are many ways to organize the portfolio. The rationale for each requirement and the documents related to the requirement may be inserted together. You could also choose to insert the rationales first and refer the reader to the requirements organized and labeled in the appendix. Consider developing a table of contents or including a table to make your organization clear.

Adapted from EDPSY 7647: Teaching for Learning in the University, *University of Missouri–St. Louis, Margaret W. Cohen, Fall 2006.*

Grading Procedures

Students are always concerned about how they will be evaluated. You can alleviate this concern by specifically describing how you test and how you assign grades. You should discuss how you evaluate written essays, homework assignments, oral presentations, labwork, and lab reports in this section of the syllabus. The section should also include the type and number of tests, their point value, and the proportion each test counts toward the final grade. Last, you should discuss how you determine the final grade. Reassure anxious students that your expectations are reasonable, fair, and attainable. Clearly articulating your standards also can reduce the chances that the overachievers will try to exert pressure on you to modify what is stated in the syllabus.

Problems concerning grades tend to prompt the most student complaints. Typical concerns include either changes in announced grading policies or differences arising from a vaguely or never-stated grading policy. A carefully thought-out policy, described in your syllabus and consistently and fairly applied, will alleviate anxiety about grades and protect you from one of the most stressful aspects of the teaching profession.

Students are eager to know not only the course requirements but also how much each of these will weigh in the final evaluation. It is important to spell out exactly how you will determine final grades. Because learning research indicates that students prepare differently for essays than for so-called objective exams, you must indicate the nature, as well as the subject matter, of the exams. Be as specific as possible about what you will cover (e.g., "Chapters 1–10, plus the lecture material") and how you will test (multiple choice, short answer, essay, etc.) so that students can prepare efficiently. Tests should be part of the learning process, reinforcing your objectives, assignments, classroom activities, and students' progress.

Your make-up policy is also critical. Inflexible policies can create ill will among students who are juggling many demands on their time. Policies that are too lenient or not specified can sometimes result in inappropriate or inconvenient student requests. Refer students to the procedures outlined in the syllabus for taking a make-up exam.

It is also helpful in this section to explain your grading rubrics and departmental expectations. Be sure to indicate whether you'll use incremental (plus/minus) grading. University policies on incomplete grades and withdrawals should also appear in this section of your syllabus. Weimer (2002) suggests that faculty members frame their grading policies on a learning-centered basis.

Example 1: Grading Criteria

Course grades: Assignments in this course will not be graded in the typical "point" fashion. Instead, you will simply be graded as pass/fail on each assignment. The number of assignments that you pass will determine your course grade.

Grade of "A"

1. Complete and hand in twelve out of fourteen possible learning logs by the due date.

2. Read and hand in summaries on eleven out of twelve possible reading assignments by the due date. Note that each reading assignment consists of two to three chapters to read and summarize.

3. Prepare and teach two chapters of your choice.

4. Complete a final project.

Grade of "B"

1. Complete and hand in eleven out of fourteen possible learning logs by the due date.

2. Read and hand in summaries on ten out of twelve possible reading assignments by the due date. Note that each reading assignment consists of two to three chapters to read and summarize.

3. Prepare and teach two chapters of your choice.

4. Complete a final project.

Grade of "C"

1. Complete and hand in ten out of fourteen possible learning logs by the due date.

2. Read and hand in summaries on nine out of twelve possible reading assignments by the due date. Note that each reading assignment consists of two to three chapters to read and summarize.

3. Prepare and teach two chapters of your choice.

Grade of "D"

1. Complete and hand in nine out of fourteen possible learning logs by the due date.

2. Read and hand in summaries on eight out of twelve possible reading assignments by the due date. Note that each reading assignment consists of two to three chapters to read and summarize.

Grade of "F"

1. Complete and hand in fewer than nine out of fourteen possible learning logs.

2. Read and summarize fewer than eight out of twelve possible reading assignments.

Adapted from Psychology 426: Advanced Physiological Psychology, *Clemson University, June Pilcher, Fall 2006.*

Example 2: Grading

Grades will be calculated and assessed as follows:

Grade	Percentage Score	Description
A	94–100%	Exemplary
A−	90–93%	Excellent
B+	87–89%	Very good
B	84–86%	Good
B−	80–83%	Satisfactory
C+	77–79%	Satisfactory
C	73–76%	Acceptable
C−	70–72%	Marginally acceptable
D+	67–69%	Marginally acceptable
D	63–66%	Pass
D−	60–62%	Minimal pass
F	Below 60%	Fail

General Grading Rubric/Criteria

A Work is complete, original, insightful, of a level and quality that significantly exceeds expectations for the student's current level of study. Products demonstrate in-depth understanding of course issues and a high level of analytical skills, are clearly and creatively presented with negligible errors in grammar and citation and source referencing, are in proper and consistent style (APA or other), and are drawn from an extensive and wide range of quality sources. Technology was explored and, where appropriate, effectively utilized in research, analysis, and presentations.

B Work is complete, of a level that meets expectations, and of a quality that is acceptable and appropriate given the student's current level of study. Products demonstrate a solid understanding of course issues and good analysis, and they are clearly and neatly presented with limited errors in grammar and citation and source referencing, in generally consistent style (APA or other), and drawn from a good range of sources. Technology was explored and, where appropriate, utilized in research, analysis, and/or presentations.

C Work is partially incomplete, late (with instructor permission/approval), and/or of a level that only partially meets expectations and/or that does not meet acceptable standards given the student's level of study. Products demonstrate inconsistent or superficial understanding of course issues with little analysis demonstrated and/or contain significant grammatical errors and incorrect/inconsistent use of citation and referencing drawn from limited and/or mixed-quality sources. Technology was minimally or inappropriately used in research, analysis, and/or presentations.

D Work is incomplete, late, and/or of a level that only partially meets expectations and/or is largely unacceptable given the student's current level of study and standing. Products demonstrate limited understanding of course issues, exhibit little analysis, and/or contain significant grammatical errors and insufficient/incorrect/inconsistent use of citation and referencing drawn from few (if any) low-quality sources. Technology was not used or inappropriately used in research, analysis, and/or presentations.

F Major assignments are missing, incomplete, or excessively late without permission of instructor or demonstrate lack of effort or lack of understanding of central course concepts.

W Withdrawal—Note that the last day to withdraw from classes with an automatic grade of "W" is November 6, 2003.

Adapted from PR 498-50: Community Development across the Globe, *Monmouth University, Bonnie Mullinix, Fall 2003.*

How to Succeed in the Course: Tools for Study and Learning

Different courses require different study patterns and practices. Include in your syllabus the strategies that you have found to work for other students who completed your course. Consider how you can help your students begin to think in the style of the discipline that you are teaching so that they develop the metacognitive tools and the framework they need to succeed in the course as they learn how to think like an historian or a solve a problem like a physicist. Refer your students to the publisher's study guides or online course supports that accompany your texts if your assessment of the supplements is that they will support learning in the course. Many supplements are written by content experts and include activities for use in class or for students' preparation for class.

Example 1: How to Study for This Course

Last, but definitely not least, think positively and believe that you can understand statistics and do well in the course. YOU ARE THE OWNER OF YOUR EDUCATION. Don't fall into the trap of telling yourself that "I'm just not a math person" or "I don't learn well in online classes." As soon as you resign yourself to these thoughts, you have lost control of the situation and may be unable to do anything to change it. If you let yourself feel that you have no control over the situation, then not only are you unable to change what happens, but how well or how much you learn is no longer your responsibility—it's out of your control. On the other hand, if you tell yourself that you can learn statistics and that you are going to take responsibility for your own learning, then you have control over the situation and can take measures to do just that. These are the same things that many of you have probably told your own students! So what are some measures that will allow you to take responsibility for your own learning?

1. Read each assigned chapter in the textbook at least three times during the week we cover the material.

2. Watch, listen, and take notes during the movies. Remember that if you do not watch the movies, it's the same as if you hadn't attended class and just got copies of the notes from someone else—you miss a lot! (Reading the PowerPoint slides does not in any way, shape, or form replace the discussion that is provided by watching and listening to the movies, regardless of your learning style.)

3. Find or form a study group with other students in the class and meet weekly to complete the homework, ask questions, and learn from your peers.

4. Find other textbooks and resources that provide different perspectives of the material, and read those each week after reading the assigned textbook reading. (There are many listed in the "resources" that can be accessed from the course content home page).

5. Complete all assigned homework during the week. Ask questions when you incorrectly answer homework problems and have trouble understanding where your understanding went awry.

6. Never, never, never get behind on readings or homework.

7. Make use of the different avenues for asking questions of peers and the instructor including posting questions on the discussion board for course content help, seeking assistance from the instructor during office hours, or making an appointment at mutually convenient times.

8. Understand that most students need to spend substantially more time on this class than any other class they have taken or are taking. Remember that you should spend three hours outside of class for every one hour that you're in class. For the weeks that we do not meet face-to-face, this means that you should be spending no less than twelve hours on the material covered in this class. For the weeks that we meet face-to-face, no less than nine hours. For students enrolled in the online section, you should be spending no less than twelve hours on the material every week. It's not uncommon for students to spend more time than that! It's essential that you are willing to commit a substantial amount of time each week to this class.

9. Think positively and continually tell yourself "I AM THE OWNER OF AND RESPONSIBLE FOR MY OWN EDUCATION. I have the ability to learn and understand statistics. I am committed to learning and understanding statistics. I am going to be proactive in learning and understanding statistics, and I will introduce strategies in my life that will ensure that I learn and understand statistics. I am responsible for my own learning, and I have control over my learning and my understanding of statistics."

10. Remember that the professor is not a mind reader. If you don't ask questions, it's assumed that you are learning and understanding the material with no problems. When you do ask questions, be clear in what you're having trouble with. Rather than just saying, "I just don't get this chapter," ask specific questions about the material that you are having trouble with. As you watch the movies, jot down the questions that you have as you go. E-mail, call, or stop by and talk with the instructor to clarify any misunderstandings.

11. Don't wait until the week before midterm to announce that you are having trouble with the material in chapter one. Remember that the material we learn is cumulative in nature—each chapter builds on the previous one. It's important that you understand the material we cover each week so that you can better learn and understand the material in the next week.

12. Likewise, don't wait until semester grades are posted at the conclusion of the semester to suddenly become concerned with your grade. Once assignments are graded and grades are posted, there is nothing that can be done. As stated on the syllabus, there is no late work, no make-up work, no re-dos, etc. It is essential that you begin taking measures and introducing strategies for success *before* you run into problems. Once assignments are submitted, it's too late.

13. Pick up and read a motivational book and remind yourself that YOU CAN DO THIS. I guarantee you that there have been students from previous semesters that have been more terrified of statistics than you, but have been committed, have taken the responsibility to learn and understand the material, have completed the class, and done well. BELIEVE IN YOURSELF. I do!

Adapted from EDF 6401: Statistics for Educational Data, *Debbie Hahs-Vaughn, University of Central Florida, Fall 2007.*

Example 2: Applying Learning Strategies to Reading the Text

In the packet of course supplements for EdPsych 312 are a variety of note-taking and learning strategies to facilitate comprehension. Traditionally, note taking for many of us was outlining. That worked well for some, but not for all, of us. There are many more strategies with which we can become familiar. Knowing how to use these paves the way to helping your future students adopt a variety of strategies as they read. As you read in Ormrod this semester, use at least six strategies once to take chapter notes. These will become part of your portfolio. I will review chapter notes periodically, checking for a variety of strategies and a demonstration that chapters have been read. After you have sampled six strategies, you are free to try others or to select those that worked especially well for you. Recognize that time constraints are such that we will not be able to address all the text in class. Nevertheless, you are responsible for reading it and demonstrating to me that you have. The supplement includes an option to the learning strategies requirement.

Excerpted from EdPsy 312: Psychology of Teaching and Learning, *University of Missouri–St. Louis, Margaret W. Cohen, Spring 2000.*

Example 3: How to Succeed in Physics

Over the many years I have spent studying physics, I have found the following approach was very effective in my study. You should try to find a way that works for you. Or maybe try my approach.

- *Preview:* You should read the textbook *before* coming to the class. Only by reading the book before the class will you be able to catch the critical concepts and ask good questions during the class.

- *During the class:* You should take good notes during the class. You do not need to copy all the stuff that I write on the blackboard—most (if not all) will be from your book. You want to write down explanations of the concepts that were confusing to you during the lectures. You can take this type of good notes only if you have read the book before you come to the class.

- *Problem solving:* The only way that you can master the concepts (and get a good grade) in physics is to solve problems, lots of problems. Because of this, I recommend the *Student Study Guide* to you. This guide contains many problems solved systematically. The most effective way to use the guide is to read a problem while covering up the solutions. Can you solve this problem? If not, take a peek at the first several lines in the solutions. Then cover it up, and try again. It does not help you if you just read this guide.

- *Tests:* Before each test, you should compile your own notes by going through the textbook, the homeworks, your class notes, and other materials. If you understand the concepts, you don't need to write down anything. If you have some difficulties in remembering the details, write down some notes to remind you. You should put this type of memory-reminds onto the one-page note that you are allowed during the test.

A Working Strategy in Solving Problems

1. Try and solve the problem yourself:
   - Draw a picture for the problem, and/or make sure that you understand what is happening in the problem.
   - Write down all the information given to you in the problem.
   - Write down all the information you need to find to solve the problem.
   - Write down the equations that you think might get you the information you need to solve the problem.
   - Plug in the numbers. Does the result make sense?

2. If you are still having difficulties:
   - Make sure you have read the text thoroughly.
   - Go through the examples in the textbook and the study guide.
   - Talk to other students in the class. Be careful here not to just follow them; it is necessary that you understand how to solve these problems to pass the class and gain understanding of the physical world around you.
   - Try again yourself, going back to the first step.

3. If you are still at a loss:

   • Come see me in my office. I will be glad to help you work through the problem or discuss any difficulties.

Adapted from Physics 24: General Physics, *University of North Carolina at Chapel Hill, Lorenza Levy, Fall 2006.*

Example 4: How to Succeed in an Online Course

Some of you might be experienced at online learning, but for others, this is your first experience with such a course. Since each of you shoulders a greater responsibility for your own learning (as well as that of your classmates) than you might in a face-to-face class, I would like to emphasize three points that I believe are critical to your success in this online version of Shaping of the Modern World.

Your personal responsibility for working on your own and exerting the personal discipline necessary to complete the assignments in a timely fashion constitutes the first point. To do this, first read the syllabus—especially the course schedule—carefully to know what to do each week, when writing assignments are due, and the date of the final examination. You will have to allow sufficient time to do the reading assignments before the dates on which postings are due. You need to include time to think about your answers and responses to questions and postings. And, you have to take an active role in the discussions we have on the course material. All of this represents a great commitment of time and effort on your part, but that is the nature of online education. Students who have taken this course previously report that there is a very direct relationship between effort and satisfaction—the more time and effort you put into the course, the more you will gain from it.

Second, I would like to emphasize the need for consistent and continual effort. All of us have a tendency (need at times) to put off work until the last minute. Doing so, I think, threatens your success in the course. You need to work on this class every day. Some of that work, like reading assignments, thinking about your answers to discussion questions, and preparing writing assignments will be done off-line. Exploring links to other relevant World Wide Web sites, posting your answers, and responding to the thoughts of others, of course, will be done online. Whatever you are working on, however, you should log on to our Blackboard site at least once a day to keep abreast of any important messages or announcements and to see how the conversations about the material we are covering at that time are developing.

The two points discussed above raise the third. Students often ask me, "How much time should I put into this course?" Obviously, that varies from one student to another, and it will vary over the eight weeks we will be working together, depending on your work and personal schedules. Based on my experience, I think you should plan to spend a minimum of six to nine hours per week on your course work. I suggest the following work schedule for the course:

Saturday through Monday: Complete assigned readings for the week, do reading in the text, explore related Web sites, and think about and plan your answers to weekly discussion questions.

Tuesday through Thursday: Post your response to the week's discussion questions (no later than 9:00 P.M. on Tuesdays) and respond to postings from other students (no later than 9:00 P.M. on Thursdays).

Friday: Take the day off; give yourself a break.

Online learning is a very different kind of experience from the traditional face-to-face class. You are more responsible for the learning you accomplish. My job is to facilitate and guide, rather than be "the sage on the stage." Working together, I am sure we can make this a significant experience for you and for the other members of the class.

Adapted from CORE 151: Shaping of the Modern World, *Duquesne University, Michael Cahall, Summer 2006.*

Example 5: How to Succeed in an Online Course

I would like to welcome you to the on-line HSC 4500 course. The format for the course will be new to most of you. The class will not meet in a traditional classroom. Since this is an introductory epidemiology course, the World Wide Web is the perfect environment for the course. We will be using several sources of media for our textbook during the semester. The main course Web site is found at: reach.ucf.edu/~hsc4500.

What do you need to be successful in the course? This is a senior level health services administration course. You must have a basic level of computer literacy. If you are not comfortable with using a PC or Mac to do your work, then don't take this course. Go back and take CGS 2100 or something similar. We will be using Microsoft Office Professional. You will need access to this to be successful. You can use it at home, work or at the campus computer labs. Microsoft Office Professional has the programs that we will be using: Word, Excel, Access, and PowerPoint. Please check the syllabus Web page for information on the book and other materials you might need.

I will be sending you e-mail before the semester begins. Included will be information to help you get off to a smooth start. It is important that your e-mail address be posted correctly; I will be using it as your official UCF address. I want to make the course as paperless as possible. Take a look at the course Web site. Check out the Syllabus, Academic Stuff, and Themes buttons. I think you will find all you need to get started. You will have the choice of reading it online or printing it out. The materials for the syllabus, academic stuff and theme Web pages should be updated on the Web sites by August 20th. The official kickoff for the course will be Friday, August 24th when add/drop is over.

The login and passwords will be set up by August 20th. Check out the instructions regarding login and passwords if you are not familiar with this. You will need to know both your PID and NID. Check out the Web site for this at: http://www.ucf.edu/pidandnid/

There are two things I need you to do right away, once you login.

1. Go to the class login (WebCT) and check out the online Calendar. Select compile and you can print out a list of all the calendar events during the semester. This is where all the information on the schedule is located.

2. Use the E-Community function to put in your correct email address, write a brief introduction, and select a picture of yourself. The E-Community button is on the main course home page. The deadline for doing this will be early in the semester. It is very important!

What is E-Community? We will be using this feature to help us build a learning community here at UCF. This allows us to post your e-mail address, write an introduction, and even post a picture. Remember that more than 80 percent of the UCF alumni stay in the Central Florida area. Your classmates are your future neighbors, partners, friends, competitors, employers, and employees. I want you to get to know each other. It's money in the bank later on!

Important information about the textbook is posted on the syllabus Web page on the course main Web site. Make sure you purchase the fourth edition of the book!

You are welcome to use the on-campus computer labs on the main campus or the regional campuses. All students at the university are given an e-mail account on the Pegasus server and access through Pegasus to the Web. You are welcome to use your PC at home or work. If you are going to use an outside Internet provider, that's fine. Internet Explorer is the recommended browser and can be downloaded for free. If you are using e-mail through sources like Yahoo or other providers, make sure your mail box does not fill up. If it does, the mail I send to you will bounce back to me and you will not know what's going on. If you do not receive e-mail from me every week, then something is not working.

During the semester, it will be necessary to check your e-mail and be online at least three times per week. You will have interaction with my teaching assistant, fellow classmates, and guests who join us. This can be done at your own convenience.

Adapted from HSC 4500: Epidemiology, *University of Central Florida, J. Stephen Lytle, Fall 2007.*

Example 6: Learning Style Inventories

Homework Due January 17, 2007

Take two learning styles inventories, VARK and the Index of Learning Styles, online. Print your results for both questionnaires. Bring your scores to the Learning Styles module on Wednesday, January 17, 2007, from 9:00 A.M. to 10:15 A.M. Failure to complete these assignments before the module will compromise your ability to participate in a discussion of how learning styles will influence your teaching and how your future students will learn most effectively.

VARK Questionnaire The VARK questionnaire aims to find out something about your preferences for the way you work with information. You will have a preferred learning style, and one part of that learning style is your preference for the intake and output of ideas and information. Choose the answer that best explains your preference, and click on the box next to the letter. Please select more than one response if a single answer does not match your perception. Leave blank any question that does not apply. You can access the VARK questionnaire at http://www.vark-learn.com/english/page.asp?p=questionnaire.

Index of Learning Styles Questionnaire The Index of Learning Styles (ILS) questionnaire consists of forty-four questions concerning your learning preferences. Answer either "a" or "b" to indicate your preference for a given item. Give only one answer per question. When you've finished, click on the "Submit" button at the end of the form.

You can access the ILS questionnaire at http://www.engr.ncsu.edu/learningstyles/ilsweb.html.

Adapted from GRAD 701: College Teaching, *University of Nevada, Reno, Barbara Millis, Lesley Sheppard, and Scott Parker, Fall 2007.*

Part III

Suggested Readings

THIS FINAL PART of the book provides a listing of published materials that focus on specific aspects of learning, teaching, and students. These readings extend the foundation provided in this guide and offer tools for thinking not only about what makes a syllabus learning centered but also about how to create learning-centered classrooms.

This bibliography has been arranged in the following categories: general teaching, active learning, assessment and evaluation, cooperative and collaborative learning, course and curriculum design, critical thinking, information technology, learning and motivation, student differences, and online resources for developing a course syllabus. It concludes with references on developing an annotated teaching portfolio to document your innovations and improvements in teaching.

General Teaching

The following volumes provide tested strategies, tips, and advice for both new and veteran college teachers.

Association of American Colleges and Universities. (2002). *Greater expectations: A new vision for learning as a nation goes to college.* Washington, DC: Author. http://greaterexpectations.org

Bain, K. (2004). *What the best college teachers do.* Cambridge, MA: Harvard University Press.

Boice, R. (1996). *First-order principles for college teachers: Ten basic ways to improve the teaching process.* Bolton, MA: Anker.

Boice, R. (2000). *Advice for new faculty members: Nihil nimus.* Boston: Allyn & Bacon.

Davis, B. G. (1993). *Tools for teaching.* San Francisco: Jossey-Bass.

Davis, J. R. (1993). *Better teaching, more learning: Strategies for success in postsecondary settings.* Phoenix, AZ: American Council on Education and Oryx Press.

Hatfield, S. R. (Ed.). (1995). *The seven principles in action: Improving undergraduate education.* Bolton, MA: Anker.

Light, R. (2001). *Making the most of college: Students speak their minds.* Cambridge, MA: Harvard University Press.

Lowman, J. (1995). *Mastering the techniques of teaching.* San Francisco: Jossey-Bass.

McKeachie, W. J., & Svinicki, M. (2005). *McKeachie's teaching tips: Strategies, research and theory for college and university teachers* (12th ed.). Boston: Houghton Mifflin.

Nilson, L. B. (2003). *Teaching at its best: A research-based resource for college instructors* (2nd ed.). Bolton, MA: Anker.

Roth, J. K. (Ed.). (1997). *Inspiring teaching: Carnegie professors of the year speak.* Bolton, MA: Anker.

Royse, D. (2001). *Teaching tips for college and university instructors.* Boston: Allyn & Bacon.

Tagg, J. (2003). *The learning paradigm college.* Bolton, MA: Anker.

Weimer, M. (2002). *Learner-centered teaching: Five key changes to practice.* San Francisco: Jossey-Bass.

Wulff, D. H. (2005). *Aligning for learning: Strategies for teaching effectiveness.* Bolton, MA: Anker.

Active Learning

These volumes offer a variety of effective active learning strategies that involve students directly in the instructional process. Suggestions for encouraging talking, listening, questioning, writing, and reflecting on course inputs are abundant and can be adapted across disciplines. Among these selections, the authors present a wide range of teaching tools, including problem-solving exercises, student projects, informal group work, simulations, case studies, and role-playing.

Bonwell, C. C., & Eison, J. A. (1991). *Active learning: Creating excitement in the classroom* (ASHE-ERIC Higher Education Report No. 1). Washington, DC: The George Washington University, School of Education and Human Development.

Meyers, C., & Jones, T. B. (1993). *Promoting active learning: Strategies for the college classroom.* San Francisco: Jossey-Bass.

Millis, B. J. (2005). Helping faculty learn to teach better and "smarter" through sequenced activities. In S. Chadwick-Blossy & D. R. Robertson (Eds.), *To improve the academy* (Vol. 24, pp. 216–230). Bolton, MA: POD Network and Anker.

Silberman, M. (1996). *Active learning: 101 strategies to teach any subject.* Boston: Allyn & Bacon.

Stanley, C., & Porter, M. E. (2002). *Engaging large classes: Strategies and techniques for college faculty.* Bolton, MA: Anker.

Sutherland, T. E., & Bonwell, C. C. (Eds.). (1996). *Using active learning in college classes: A range of options for faculty.* San Francisco: Jossey-Bass.

Assessment and Evaluation

The first book that follows on classroom assessment techniques is regarded as a classic and includes a helpful Teaching Goals Inventory to identify and clarify instructional goals. Each of the other titles offers detailed suggestions and advice on planning, designing, and implementing a variety of classroom assessment strategies.

Angelo, T. A., & Cross, K. P. (1993). *Classroom assessment techniques: A handbook for college teachers.* San Francisco: Jossey-Bass.

Huba, M. E., & Freed, J. E. (2000). *Learner-centered assessment on college campuses: Shifting the focus from teaching to learning.* Needham Heights, MA: Allyn & Bacon.

Walvoord, B. E. (2004). *Assessment clear and simple: A practical guide for institutions, departments, and general education.* San Francisco: Jossey-Bass.

Walvoord, B. E., & Anderson, V. J. (1998). *Effective grading: A tool for learning and assessment.* San Francisco: Jossey-Bass.

Cooperative and Collaborative Learning

Cooperative learning refers to the instructional use of highly structured small groups (teams) in which students work together to maximize their own and each others' learning, often through problem-solving activities. Key principles are (1) positive interdependence (students have a vested reason to work together, usually dictated by the nature of the task); (2) individual accountability (students receive grades that reflect their own efforts and achievements rather than receiving a group grade that doesn't differentiate among contributions); (3) heterogeneity in team composition (not a "given" in the literature, but necessary to promote critical thinking that comes from divergent thinking. It also helps group members question assumptions and build work place skills that encourage students to work cooperatively with students unlike themselves); (4) group processing (both the students and the teacher pay attention to what goes on in the groups/ teams); and (5) social skills (basically workplace skills such as leadership skills and facilitation skills to draw out contributions from all team members, etc.). Collaborative learning is not as specifically defined. The selections here offer a variety of research-based conceptual approaches and general principles for considering how to structure cooperative learning activities based on the discipline, curriculum, students, and setting.

Barkley, E. F., Cross, K. P., & Major, C. H. (2005). *Collaborative learning techniques: A handbook for college faculty.* San Francisco: Jossey-Bass.

Cooper, J. L., Robinson, P., & Ball, D. (2003). *Small group instruction in higher education: Lessons from the past, visions of the future.* Stillwater, OK: New Forums Press.

Johnson, D. W., Johnson, R. T., & Smith, K. A. (1998). *Active learning: Cooperation in the college classroom.* Edina, MN: Interaction Book.

Miller, J. E., Groccia, J. E., & Miller, M. S. (2001). *Student-assisted teaching: A guide to faculty-student teamwork.* Bolton, MA: Anker.

Millis, B. J. (2002, October). *Enhancing learning—and more!—through cooperative learning* (IDEA Paper No. 38). Manhattan: Kansas State University, IDEA Center. Retrieved July, 7, 2006, from http://www.idea.k-state.edu/resources/index.html

Millis, B. J., & Cottell, P. G., Jr. (1998). *Cooperative learning for higher education faculty.* Phoenix, AZ: American Council on Education and Oryx Press.

Course and Curriculum Design

The authors of the volumes that follow are masterful in describing curricular changes with which they've been involved and in offering guidelines for various phases of planning, designing, and assessing a curriculum. In each, case studies and actual examples are included as practical applications of how faculty from a variety of disciplines have revised and revitalized their curricula.

Diamond, R. M. (1998). *Designing and assessing courses and curricula: A practical guide.* San Francisco: Jossey-Bass.

Fink, L. D. (2003). *Creating significant learning experiences: An integrated approach to designing college courses.* San Francisco: Jossey-Bass.

Gardiner, L. F. (1994). *Redesigning higher education: Producing dramatic gains in student learning* (ASHE-ERIC Higher Education Report, No. 7). San Francisco: Jossey-Bass.

Jenrette, M. S., & Napoli, V. (1994). *The teaching/learning enterprise: Miami-Dade community college's blueprint for change.* Bolton, MA: Anker.

Lunde, J. P. (Ed.). (1995). *Reshaping curricula: Revitalization programs at three land grant universities.* Bolton, MA: Anker.

Wiggins, G., & McTighe, J. (2005). *Understanding by design.* (2nd ed.). Alexandria, VA: Association for Supervision and Curriculum Development.

Critical Thinking

These resources review the research on how faculty can help students develop critical thinking skills in the higher education classroom. Each suggests strategies for blending critical thinking into content learning. Taken together, the two books offer a broad array of examples that can be adapted to increase critical thinking in assignments, instruction, courses, and programs.

Bean, J. C. (1996). *Engaging ideas: The professor's guide to integrating writing, critical thinking, and active learning in the classroom.* San Francisco: Jossey-Bass.

Kurfiss, J. G. (1988). *Critical thinking: Theory, research, practice and possibilities* (ASHE-ERIC Higher Education Report, No. 2). San Francisco: Jossey-Bass.

Nelson, C. E. (1999). On the persistence of unicorns: The trade-off between content and critical thinking revisited. In B. Pescosolido & R. Aminzade (Eds.). *The social worlds of higher education: Handbook for teaching in a new century* (pp. 168–184). Thousand Oaks, CA: Pine Forge Press.

Information Technology

Although a broad array of published materials is available about how to use information technology as a tool for teaching and learning, the selections here are recommended because they offer direction for creating effective online learning environments. Moving a course from the face-to-face classroom to an online environment requires a radical revision of instructional strategies and course requirements in order to ensure that students are focused on learning. Guiding students to adopt successful learning strategies online is paramount to the success of an online course. These resources provide conceptual and practical direction.

Bates, A. W., & Poole, G. (2003). *Effective teaching with technology in higher education: Foundations for success.* San Francisco, Jossey-Bass.

Bonk, C. J., & Graham, C. R. (2006). *Handbook of blended learning: Global perspectives/ local designs.* San Francisco: Wiley.

Chickering, A. W., & Ehrmann, S. C. (1996). Implementing the seven principles: Technology as a lever. *AAHE Bulletin.* (pp. 3–6). http://www.tltgroup.org/programs/seven.html.

Conrad, R. M., & Donaldson, J. A. (2004). *Engaging the online learner: Activities and resources for creative instruction.* San Francisco: Jossey-Bass.

Madigan, D. (2006, March). *The technology literate professoriate: Are we there yet?* (IDEA Paper No. 43). Manhattan: Kansas State University, IDEA Center. Retrieved December 31, 2006, from http://www.idea.ksu.edu/papers/Idea_Paper_43.pdf

National Association of College Stores & the Association of American Publishers. (2007). *Questions and answers on copyright for the campus community.* New York: Author.

Learning and Motivation

These selections synthesize recent research in cognition, learning, and motivation by leading the reader to understand the implications of the research for curricular and instructional processes.

Bransford, J., Brown, A. L., & Cocking, R. (Eds.). (2000). *How people learn: Brain, mind, experience, and school.* Washington, DC: National Academies Press.

Leamnson, R. (1999). *Thinking about teaching and learning: Developing habits of learning with first year college and university students.* Sterling, VA: Stylus.

Sousa, D. A. (2001). *How the brain learns.* Thousand Oaks, CA: Corwin Press.

Svinicki, M. (2004). *Learning and motivation in the postsecondary classroom.* Bolton, MA: Anker.

Zull, J. E. (2002). *The art of changing the brain: Enriching the practice of teaching by exploring the biology of learning.* Sterling, VA: Stylus.

Student Differences

Social and cultural differences can affect students' preparation, expectations, and needs for learning in a college environment. These sources will help you understand the broad patterns of student learning and development that influence students' responses to learning situations. They will help you guide your students as they struggle to understand their own particular styles of learning. Because the topic of individual differences refers to a vast array of variables, brief annotations are included for each source.

Belenky, M. F., Clinchy, B. M., Goldberger, N. R., & Tarule, J. M. (1986). *Women's ways of knowing: The development of self, voice, and mind.* New York: Basic Books.

> This classic in the field offers illuminating explanations of positions or perspectives of intellectual and ethical development in student thinking. Belenky and her colleagues argue that women develop along different intellectual lines from men because of different value orientations.

Ericksen, S. C., & Strommer, D. W. (1991). *Teaching college freshmen.* San Francisco: Jossey-Bass.

> Drawing on freshman learning research, the authors offer practical guidance on how to teach and provide academic support for

students during the crucial first year. They examine students' diverse educational backgrounds, learning styles, expectations about learning, educational goals, and values. After identifying anxieties, habits, and assumptions that can impede learning progress, they present strategies for overcoming these obstacles.

Gardner, H. (2006). *Multiple intelligences: New horizons.* (2nd ed.). New York: Basic Books.

> Gardner's innovative analysis of how people learn reveals many types of intelligences that can guide instructors to create relevant strategies that maximize learning and engagement. Gardner proposes that when a teacher makes available several entry points at the beginning of a learning opportunity and over time, there is a good chance that students with differing intelligence profiles will find relevant and meaningful ways of learning.

Friedman, E. G., Kolmar, W. K., Flint, C. B., & Rothenberg, P. (Eds.). (1996). *Creating an inclusive classroom: A teaching sourcebook from the New Jersey Project.* New York: Teachers College Press.

> This volume gathers over forty innovative syllabi, teaching resources, and reflective essays intended to move college curricula toward being inclusive, nonsexist, nonracist, and multicultural.

Kolb, D. A. (1985). *Learning style inventory.* Boston: McBer.

> The author identifies a learning cycle grounded in an experiential model of learning. The four phases of the cycle—concrete experience, reflective observation, abstract conceptualization, and active experimentation—each require different processes to acquire different information and to learn different skills.

Perry, W. G., Jr. (1970). *Forms of intellectual and ethical development in the college years.* San Francisco: Jossey-Bass.

> Perry's work offers a developmental study of Harvard students (all white males) during the course of their undergraduate years.

Wlodkowski, R. J., & Ginsberg, M. B. (1995). *Diversity and motivation: Culturally responsive teaching.* San Francisco: Jossey-Bass.

> This volume offers guidance and suggestions for respectful teaching practices that cross disciplines and cultures. Using a motivational framework that applies culturally responsive teaching to the postsecondary setting, the authors describe learning strategies and structures necessary to establish inclusion, enhance meaning, and engender competence. An analysis of a syllabus is included to

show how the syllabus is consistent with norms, procedures, and structures of culturally responsive teaching and where improvements are possible.

Online Resources for Syllabus Construction

The Web resources constructed by the professional development centers for faculty and teaching assistants on college and university campuses provide current and creative suggestions, templates, and ideas for teaching and learning. The sources that follow have particularly helpful documents and supports for developing a syllabus.

Arizona State University, Center for Learning and Teaching Excellence, *Syllabus design,* http://www.asu.edu/upfd/syllabus

Brown University, Sheridan Center for Teaching and Learning. *Constructing a syllabus,* http://www.brown.edu/Administration/Sheridan_Center/publications/syllabus.html (prepared by Michael J.V. Woolcock).

Duquesne University, Center for Teaching Excellence, *Syllabus checklist,* http://www.cte.duq.edu/resources/TchInstruction/eResources/syllabuschecklistrev.html (prepared by Laurel Willingham-McLain).

Iowa State University, Center for Teaching and Learning, *Learning-centered syllabi workshop,* http://www.cte.iastate.edu/tips/syllabi.html (prepared by Lee Haugen).

Nuhfer, E. *Nutshell notes: Building a better syllabus,* http://profcamp.tripod.com/nnbootmaster.pm.pdf.

Park University, *Creating a syllabus,* http://www.park.edu/cetl/quicktips/

St. Edward's University (Austin, TX), Center for Teaching Excellence, *Syllabus construction,* http://www.stedwards.edu/cte/content/view/1517/49/

University of Massachusetts Lowell, Faculty Teaching Center, *Learning-centered teaching,* http://www.uml.edu/centers/FTC/lct.html

University of Missouri–St. Louis, Center for Teaching and Learning, *Essential elements of a syllabus,* http://www.umsl.edu/services/ctl/instr_support/tchng_res.html (prepared by Margaret W. Cohen and updated in 2007).

Western Illinois University, Provost's Office, *Course syllabus,* http://www.wiu.edu/users/miprov/facpol/acad/syllabus.htm

Teaching Portfolios

Your learning-centered syllabus can serve as a significant document in your professional portfolio as evidence of innovation and significant improvement in the quality of your teaching. The following provide guides for constructing and using teaching portfolios.

Bernstein, D., Burnett, A. N., Goodburn, A., & Savory, P. (2006). *Making teaching and learning visible: Course portfolios and the peer review of teaching.* Bolton, MA: Anker.

Seldin, P. (2004). *The teaching portfolio: A practical guide to improved performance and promotional/tenure decisions* (3rd ed.). Bolton, MA: Anker.

Seldin, P., & Associates. (1993). *Successful use of teaching portfolios.* Bolton, MA: Anker.

Zubizarreta, J. (2004). *The learning portfolio: Reflective practice for improving student learning.* Bolton, MA: Anker.

References

Albers, C. (2003). Using the syllabus to document the scholarship of teaching. *Teaching Sociology, 31*, 60–72.

Angelo, T. A., & Cross, K. P. (1993). *Classroom assessment techniques: A handbook for college teachers.* San Francisco: Jossey-Bass.

Association of American Colleges and Universities. (2002). *Greater expectations: A new vision for learning as a nation goes to college.* Retrieved June 16, 2007, from http://greaterexpectations.org

Association of College & Research Libraries. (2006). *Standards and Guidelines.* Retrieved January 1, 2007, from http://www.ala.org/acrl/guides

Bain, K. (2004). *What the best college teachers do.* Cambridge, MA: Harvard University Press.

Banta, T. W., & Kuh, G. D. (1998). A missing link in assessment: Collaboration between academic and student affairs professionals. *Change, 30*(2), 40–46.

Barkley, E. F., Cross, K. P., & Major, C. H. (2005). *Collaborative learning techniques: A handbook for college faculty.* San Francisco: Jossey-Bass.

Baron, L. (2001, August). Why information literacy?: Empowering teachers and students in the classroom and beyond. *Advocate Online, 18*(8). Retrieved June 21, 2007, from http://www2.nea.org/he/advo01/advo0108/front.html

Barr, R. B., & Tagg, J. (1995). From teaching to learning: A new paradigm for undergraduate education. *Change, 27*(6), 12–25.

Bauerlein, M. (2006, January 6). A very long disengagement. *Chronicle of Higher Education,* pp. B6–B8.

Bean, J. C. (1996). *Engaging ideas: The professor's guide to integrating writing, critical thinking, and active learning in the classroom.* San Francisco: Jossey-Bass.

Beichner, R. (2006, January 30). *Making the case for interaction.* Paper presented at the annual meeting of the Educause Learning Initiative, San Diego, CA. Retrieved November 23, 2007, http://www.educause.edu/ir/library/pdf/ELI0602.pdf

Black, B. (1998). Using the SGID method for a variety of purposes. In M. Kaplan (Ed.), *To improve the academy: Resources for faculty, instructional, and organizational development* (Vol. 17, pp. 245–262). Stillwater, OK: New Forums Press and the Professional and Organizational Development Network in Higher Education.

Bonwell, C. C., & Eison, J. A. (1991). *Active learning: Creating excitement in the classroom* (ASHE-ERIC Higher Education Report No. 1). Washington, DC: The George Washington University, School of Education and Human Development.

Bozik, M., & Tracey, K. (2002). Fostering intellectual development in a learning community: Using an electronic bulletin board. In P. Comeaux (Ed.), *Communication and collaboration in the online classroom* (pp. 207–225). Bolton, MA: Anker.

Bransford, J. D., Brown, A. L., & Cocking, R. R. (Eds.). (2000). *How people learn: Brain, mind, experience, and school.* Washington, DC: National Academies Press.

Brown, A. L., Ash, D., Rutherford, M., Nakagawa, K., Gordon, A., & Campione, J. C. (1993). Distributed expertise in the classroom. In G. Salomon (Ed.), *Distributed cognitions: Psychological and educational considerations.* Cambridge, England: Cambridge University Press.

Byington, E. (2002). Communicating: The key to success in an online writing and reading course. In P. Comeaux (Ed.), *Communication and collaboration in the online classroom* (pp. 192–206). Bolton, MA: Anker.

Carlson, S. (2005, October 7). The Net generation in the classroom. *Chronicle of Higher Education*, pp. A34–A37.

Chickering, A. W., & Gamson, Z. F. (1987). Seven principles for good practice in undergraduate education. *AAHE Bulletin, 39*(7), 3–7.

Chism, N.V.N. (1998). Developing a philosophy of teaching statement. *Essays on Teaching Excellence, 9*(3), 1–2. Professional and Organizational Development Network in Higher Education. Retrieved June 17, 2007, http://ftad.osu.edu/portfolio/philosophy/Philosophy.html

Colby, A., Ehrlich, T., Beaumont, E., & Stephens, J. (2003). *Educating citizens: Preparing America's undergraduates for lives of moral and civic responsibility.* San Francisco: Jossey-Bass.

Collins, T. (1997). For openers . . . An inclusive syllabus. In W. F. Campbell & K. A. Smith (Eds.), *New paradigms for college teaching* (pp. 79–102). Edina, MN: Interaction Book.

Copyright Act of 1976, Public Law 94–553, 94th Cong. (August 19, 1976).

Davis, B. G. (1993). *Tools for teaching.* San Francisco: Jossey-Bass.

Davis, J. R. (1993). *Better teaching, more learning: Strategies for success in postsecondary settings.* Phoenix, AZ: American Council on Education and Oryx Press.

Dembo, M. H. (2004). *Motivation and learning strategies for college success: A self-management approach* (2nd ed.). Mahwah, NJ: Erlbaum.

Donovan, M. S., & Bransford, J. D. (2005). *How students learn: History, mathematics, and science in the classroom.* Washington, DC: National Academies Press.

Downing, S. (2005). *On course: Strategies for creating success in college and in life.* Boston: Houghton Mifflin.

Fink, L. D. (2003). *Creating significant learning experiences: An integrated approach to designing college courses.* San Francisco: Jossey-Bass.

Finkle, D. (2000). *Teaching with your mouth shut.* Portsmouth, NH: Heinemann.

Goodyear, G., & Allchin, D. (1998). Statements of teaching philosophy. Retrieved June 17, 2007, from http://sunconference.utep.edu/CETaL/resources/stofteach.html

Groccia, J. (1997, May/June). The student as customer versus the student as learner. *About Campus,* 31–32.

Harris, M., & Cullen, R. (2007, May). Civic engagement and curricular reform. *National Teaching and Learning Forum, 16*(4), 4–6.

Heiman, M., & Slomianko, J. (2003). *Learning to learn: Thinking skills for the 21st century* (10th ed.). Cambridge, MA: Learning to Learn.

Huba, M. E., & Freed, J. E. (2000). *Learner-centered assessment on college campuses: Shifting the focus from teaching to learning.* Boston: Allyn & Bacon.

Jensen, E. (2000). *Teaching with the brain in mind.* Washington, DC: Association for Supervision and Curriculum Development.

Kuh, G. D. (2003). What we're learning about engagement from NSSE: Bookmarks for effective educational practices. *Change, 35*(2), 24–32.

Kuh, G. D. (2007, June 15). How to help students achieve. *Chronicle of Higher Education,* pp. B12–13.

Kuh, G. D., Kinzie, J., Schuh, J. H., Whitt, E. J., & Associates. (2005). *Student success in college: Creating conditions that matter.* San Francisco: Jossey-Bass.

Kurfiss, J. G. (1988). *Critical thinking: Theory, research, practice and possibilities* (ASHE-ERIC Higher Education Report No. 2). Washington, DC: Association for the Study of Higher Education.

Lough, J. R. (1997). The Carnegie professors of the year: Models for teaching success. In J. Roth (Ed.), *Inspiring teaching: Carnegie professors of the year speak.* Bolton, MA: Anker.

Marton, F., Hounsell, D., & Entwistle, N. J. (1997). *The experience of learning* (2nd ed.). Edinburgh, Scotland: Scottish Academic Press.

McCormick, A., & Zhao, C. (2005). Rethinking and reframing the Carnegie classification. *Change, 37*(5), 52–57.

McGuire, S. Y., & Williams, D. A. (2002). The millennial learner: Challenges and opportunities. In D. Lieberman (Ed.), *To improve the academy: Resources for faculty, instructional, and organizational development* (Vol. 20, pp. 185–196). Bolton, MA: Anker.

Millis, B. J., & Cottell, P. G. (1998). *Cooperative learning for higher education faculty.* Phoenix: American Council on Education and Oryx Press.

Nilson, L. B. (2002). The graphic syllabus: Shedding a visual light on course organization. In D. Lieberman (Ed.), *To improve the academy: Resources for faculty, instructional, and organizational development* (Vol. 20, pp. 238–259). Bolton, MA: Anker.

Nilson, L. B. (2003). *Teaching at its best: A research-based resource for college instructors* (2nd ed.). Bolton, MA: Anker.

Noyd, R. K. (2004, Spring). Notetakers, content, and effective instruction: Pros, cons, what works, and what doesn't. *USAFA Educator, 12*(2), 4–5.

Nuhfer, E., & Knipp, D. (2003). The knowledge survey: A tool for all reasons. In D. H. Wulff & J. D. Nyquist (Eds.), *To improve the academy: Resources for faculty, instructional, and organizational development* (Vol. 21, pp. 50–78). Stillwater, OK: New Forums Press. Retrieved June 22, 2007, from http://www.isu.edu/ctl/facultydev/KnowS_files/KnowS.htm

Oblinger, D. G. (2003, July/August). Boomers, gen-Xers, and Millennials: Understanding the "new students." *Educause Review, 38*(4), 36–40, 42, 44–45.

Oblinger, D. G., & Hawkins, B. L. (2005, July/August). IT myths: The myth about e-learning. *Educause Review, 40*(4), 14–15.

Oblinger, D. G., & Oblinger, J. (2006). Is it age or IT? First steps toward understanding the Net generation. *California School Library Association Journal, 29*(2), 8–16.

Ouimet, J. (2007, October 16–17). *Engagement: A CLASSE act.* Paper presented at the Regional NSSE Users Workshop, University of Nevada, Reno.

Polyson, S., Saltzberg, S., & Godwin-Jones, R. (1996, September). A practical approach to teaching with the World Wide Web. *Syllabus,* 12–16.

Redmond, M. V., & Clark, D. J. (1982). A practical approach to improving teaching. *AAHE Bulletin, 34*(6), 8–10.

Rhem, J. (1995). Deep/surface approaches to learning: An introduction. *National Teaching and Learning Forum, 5*(1), 1–4.

Rhem, J. (2007). CLASSE—The missing link? *National Teaching and Learning Forum. 16*(4), 1–3.

Rocheleau, J., & Speck, B. W. (2007). *Rights and wrongs in the college classroom: Ethical issues in postsecondary teaching.* Bolton, MA: Anker.

Seldin, P. (1998). How colleges evaluate teaching: 1988 vs. 1998. *AAHE Bulletin, 50*(7), 3–7.

Seldin, P. (2004). *The teaching portfolio* (3rd ed.). Bolton, MA: Anker.

Seldin, P. (2007, April 13). *Evaluating college teaching: New lessons learned.* Paper presented at Lilly-East Conference on College and University Teaching, University of Delaware, Newark, DE.

Shulman, L. S. (2004). From idea to prototype: Three exercises in peer review. (Originally published 1995.) In *Teaching as community property: Essays on higher education.* San Francisco: Jossey-Bass.

Silberman, M. (1996). *Active learning: 101 strategies to teach any subject.* Des Moines, IA: Prentice Hall.

Smallwood, R. (2007, October 16–17). *CLASSE: A measure of student engagement at the classroom level.* Paper presented at the Regional NSSE Users Workshop, University of Nevada, Reno.

Smith, R. M., & Stalcup, K. A. (2001). Technology consulting: Keeping pedagogy in the forefront. In K. G. Lewis & J.T.P. Lunde (Eds.), *Face to face: A sourcebook of individual consultation techniques for faculty/instructional developers* (pp. 227–245). Stillwater, OK: New Forums Press.

Strauss, W., & Howe, N. (2005, October 21). The high cost of college: An increasingly hard sell. *Chronicle of Higher Education,* p. B24. Retrieved July 8, 2007, from http://chronicle.com/weekly/v52/i09/09b02401.htm

Streck, P. (2007). If you only had your students for a week, what would you want them to learn? Part I. *National Teaching and Learning Forum, 16*(4), 8–9.

Svinicki, M. D. (2004). *Learning and motivation in the postsecondary classroom.* Bolton, MA: Anker.

Tagg, J. (2003). *The learning paradigm college.* Bolton, MA: Anker.

Weimer, M. (2002). *Learner-centered teaching: Five key changes to practice.* San Francisco: Jossey-Bass.

Wiggins, G., & McTighe, J. (2005). *Understanding by design* (2nd ed.). Alexandria, VA: Association for Supervision and Curriculum Development.

Wilhite, M. S., Lunde, J.T.P., & King, J. W. (2001). Consultation for distance teaching. In K. G. Lewis & J.T.P. Lunde (Eds.), *Face to face: A sourcebook of individual consultation techniques for faculty/instructional developers* (pp. 247–272). Stillwater, OK: New Forums Press.

Windham, C. (2007, May/June). Confessions of a podcast junkie. *Educause Review,* 51–65.

Wlodkowski, R. J., & Ginsberg, M. B. (1995). *Diversity and motivation: Culturally responsive teaching.* San Francisco: Jossey-Bass.

Worrall, P., & Kline, B. (2002). Building a communications learning community. In P. Comeaux (Ed.), *Communication and collaboration in the online classroom* (pp. 226–241). Bolton, MA: Anker.

Wulff, D. H., & Nyquist, J. D. (1986). Using qualitative methods to generate data for instructional development. *To improve the academy: Resources for faculty, instructional, and organizational development* (Vol. 5). Stillwater, OK: New Forums Press, 37–46.

Index

A

Academic honesty, 88–90
Active learning: describing, 28–29; and good practice, 46; identifying and assembling resources for, 19–21; and structuring students' active involvement in learning, 18–19; suggested readings on, 112–113
Active Learning Site, 28
Albers, C., 6
Allchin, D., 6
Angelo, T. A., 13, 92–93
Appreciating, 14
Aronson, A., 75, 76
Arróyave, R., 90
Assessment: measures, 16–17; philosophical norms for, 17; suggested readings in, 113
Association of American Colleges and Universities, 1–3, 5
Association of College and Research Libraries, 3
Attendance policy, 78–79
Auburn University, 62
Australia, 12

B

Bach, J.P.G., 63
Backwards design model, 14
Bain, K., 11, 28
Barkley, E. F., 1
Barnes, R., 60, 80
Baron, L., 3
Barr, R. B., 1
Basic statistics, 65
Bauerlein, M., 2

Bean, J. C., 19
Beaumont, E., 34
Behavioral science, 65–66
Beichner, R., 4
Berk, R. A., 43, 66
Black, B., 37
Blackboard, 22, 26, 27, 35, 107
Boise State University, 63
Bonwell, C. C., 28
Bozik, M., 31
Bransford, J. D., 4, 12, 13, 33, 92
Brown, A. L., 4, 12, 13, 20, 33, 92
Building Models to Solve Engineering Problems (University Honors College, University of Minnesota), 42
Byington, E., 31

C

Cahall, M., 108
Campus crisis preparedness, 91
Campus safety, 91–92
Carlson, S., 2
Carnegie classification comparator group, 8
Center for Teaching and Learning, 43
CGI, 24
Chadick, P., 54
Checklist, syllabus preparation, 39–40
Chickering, A. W., 9, 45
Chism, N.V.N., 6
Civil behaviors, 80–81
Civility, 84–85; statements of, 7
Clark, D. J., 37

Class: conduct in, 84; ground rules, 81–82; make-up policy, 78–79

CLASSE. *See* "Classroom Survey of Student Engagement"

Clemson University, 101

Clickers, 21, 65

Cocking, R. R., 4, 12, 13, 33, 92

Cohen, M. W., 43, 86, 91, 98, 105

Colby, A., 34

Collaborative reading, suggested readings in, 113–114

Collins, T., 44

Columbia College, 57, 90

Conceptual framework, 30

Connecticut College, 85

Cooperative group work, 13; suggested readings in, 113–114

Copyright Act of 1976, 20

Copyright Clearance Center, 21

Copyrighted material, 20–21

Cottell, P. G., 12, 33

Course: content, 18; defining student responsibilities for successful work in, 28; helping students assess readiness for, 29; logistics of, 27; role of technology in, 30–31; setting, in broader context for learning, 29–30; setting tone for, 26; suggested reading in design of, 114

Course calendar, 67–71; example 1, 69–70; example 2, 70–71

Course description, 51–54; example 1, 51–52; example 2, 52–53; example 3, 53–54

Course objectives, 54–63; example 1, 55–57; example 2, 57–58; example 3, 58–59; example 4, 59–60; example 5, 60–62; example 6, 62–63; four basic questions for, 54–55

Course purpose, 49–51; example 1, 49; example 2, 49–50; example 3, 50–51

Course requirements, 71–77; example 1 (class participation), 71–72; example 2 (class participation), 72–73; example 3 (working in groups), 73–75; example 4 (working in groups), 75–76; example 5 (group work in problem-based learning), 76–77

Course success: and applying learning strategies to reading text, 105; and how to study for course, 103–105; and how to succeed in online course, 107–110; and how to succeed in physics, 105–107; and learning style inventories, 110; tools for, 102–110

Creating Significant Learning Experiences (Fink), 2

Creighton University, 77

Critical thinking, 19; suggested readings in, 115

Crosby-Currie, C., 50

Cross, K. P., 1, 13, 92–93

Cullen, R., 2

Curriculum design, suggested readings in, 114

D

Davis, B. G., 4, 18

Davis, J. R., 17–19

Deep learning, 10, 12, 13, 33

Delmonico, J., 84

Dembo, M. H., 32

Disabilities statement, 90–91

Disability access, 7

Disciplinary societies, 7

Diverse talents, 46

Donovan, M. S., 13

Downing, S., 32

Duneczky, C., 58, 91

Duquesne University, 70, 108

E

Educational purposes, beliefs about, 26–27

Ehrlich, T., 34

Eison, J. A., 28

Electronic discussion boards, 31

Entwistle, N. J., 12

Evaluation, 92–98; essay for, 93–94; and learning contract, 97–98; and peer assessment, 94–95; suggested readings in, 113

Expectations: clarifying, 5–8; and good practice, 46; and responsibilities and policies, 6–8

F

Faculty responsibilities, 83–84

Family Educational Rights and Privacy Act, 26

Fayetteville State University, 11

Feedback, good practice and, 46

Felkey, B., 62

Fink, L. D., 2, 14, 92

Finkle, D., 4

Flash, 24

Frary, M., 63

Freed, J. E., 16–17

"From Teaching to Learning: A New Paradigm for Undergraduate Education" (Barr and Tagg), 1
Frostburg University, 78

G

Gamson, Z. F., 9, 45
General teaching, suggested readings on, 111–112
Ginsberg, M. B., 17, 36, 37
Godwin-Jones, R., 31
Good practice, 45–46
Goodyear, G., 6
Grading procedures, 98–102; criteria for, 99–101; rubric for, 101–102
Grant, R., 80
Gratton, K., 58, 91
Great Britain, 12
Greater Expectations: A New Vision for Learning as a Nation Goes to College (Association of American Colleges and Universities), 1–2
Groccia, J., 9

H

Hahn, N., 64
Hahs-Vaughn, D., 105
Han, P-C., 98
Handouts, 27–28
Harris, M., 2
Hawkins, B. L., 25
Heiman, M., 32
Henschke, J., 98
Hobson, E. H., 33
Horwitz, S., 50
Hounsell, D., 12
How People Learn (Bransford, Brown, and Cocking), 4
How Students Learn: History, Mathematics, and Science in the Classroom (Donovan and Bransford), 13
Howe, N., 2
Huba, M. E., 16–17
Huckaby, M. F., 41
Hypertext mark-up language (HTML), 23, 24

I

ILS. *See* Index of Learning Styles
Index of Learning Styles (ILS), 110
Information literacy, 3

Information technology, suggested reading in, 115–116
Instructor information: example 1, 41–42; example 2, 42–43; example 3, 43
Interaction with others, 12

J

Java, 24
JavaScript, 24
Jensen, E., 13
Jensen, G., 77
Johns Hopkins University, 66; School of Nursing, 43
Johnson County Community College, 46, 58, 67, 91

K

Kavookjian, J., 62
Kehrwald, K., 78
King, J. W., 23
Kinzie, J., 10, 11, 25
Kline, B., 31
Knipp, D., 29
Knowledge base, well-structured, 12
Knowledge framework: and clarifying expectations, 5–8; and expectations, responsibilities, and policies, 6–8; and inclusion of teaching philosophy, 6; setting, 4–13
Knowledge-based economy, 3
Kothmann, M. M., 73
Krise, T., 88
Kuh, G. D., 1, 9–11, 25
Kurfiss, J. G., 18, 19

L

Learner activity, 12
Learning, 4; acknowledging context for, 9–11; deep, 10, 12, 13, 33; demonstration of, 17; encouraging responsibility for, 8–9; focus on, 1–38; outside classroom, 33; structuring active involvement in, 18–19; suggested reading, 116; surface, 12
Learning contract, 33–34, 97–98
Learning Paradigm College, The (Tagg), 1
Learning resources, available, 30
Learning-centered perspective, 4
Learning-centered syllabus: composing, 21–34; content of, 21–22; and deciding on desired outcomes and assessment measures, 16–17; and

Learning-centered syllabus (*Continued*)
defining and delimiting course content, 18; developing, 11–13; and developing well-grounded rationale for course, 15; form of, 22–23; four key components of, 12; online, 23–25; planning, 13–21; and structuring students' active involvement in learning, 18–19; three stages of planning, 14; using, 34–37
Learning-Centered Teaching (Weimer), 2
Learningtolearn.com, 32
Lennox, C., 70
Letter to student, 44–49; example 1, 45–46
Levy, L., 107
Liberal arts curriculum, 2
Lotus Notes, 31
Lough, J. R., xii
Lunde, J.T.P., 23
Lytle, J. S., 110

M

Major, C. H., 1
Marton, F., 12
Matthews, M., 84
McCormick, A., 8
McGuire, S. Y., 2
McLain, L. W., 70
McTighe, J., 14, 18
Metropolitan State University, 75, 76, 81, 94
Microsoft, 23–24
Microsoft Exchange, 31
Millenials, 2, 9, 31
Millis, B. J., 12, 33, 54, 88, 110
Miss America, 19
Missouri State University, 92
Mohr, E., 46, 67
Monmouth University, 88, 97, 102
Morrison, T., 66
Motivation, suggested reading, 116
Motivational content, 12
Mullinix, B., 88, 97, 102

N

National Survey of Student Engagement (NSSE), 9, 10, 25, 31
Nerney, B., 94
New Mexico Junior College, 91
Nilson, L. B., 14, 15
Northern Arizona University, 66

Note taking, 32
Noyd, R. K., 32
NSSE. *See* National Survey of Student Engagement (NSSE)
Nuhfer, E., 29
Nyquist, J. D., 37

O

Oblinger, D. G., 9, 24, 25
Oblinger, J., 24
Ouimet, J., 10
Outcomes, desired, 16–17

P

Parker, S., 110
Parks, Bert, 19
PDF. *See* Portable document format
Pedagogy, learning-centered, 2
Peer assessment, 94–95
Pfeiffer, R., 42, 43, 47, 59
Pilcher, J., 101
Point of contact, early, 25–26
Policies and expectations, 6–8, 77–92; and academic honesty, 88–90; and attendance and class make-up policy, 78–79; and attendance policy, 78; and campus crisis preparedness, 91; and campus safety, 91–92; and class ground rules, 81–82; and classroom conduct, 84; and disabilities statement, 90–91; and expectations for civil behaviors, 80–81; and expectations for professional behaviors, 79–80; and expectations for rational and intellectual discussion, 80; and faculty responsibilities, 83–84; and participation and civility, 84–85; and preparation for course success, 85–86; and responsibilities, 81–84; and safety, 91; and student responsibilities, 82–83; and using wireless technologies in class, 86–87
Polyson, S., 31
Portable document format (PDF), 23
PowerPoint, 32
Pro-Con-Caveat Grid, 33
Professional behaviors, 79–80

Q

Questionnaire, 37

R

Reading materials, difficult-to-obtain, 32
Reder, M., 85
Rediehs, L., 72, 79

Redmond, M. V., 37

Resources, 65–67; about community or cultural contexts, 66; basic statistics, 65; behavioral science, 65–66; on classroom settings, 66; on statistical power analysis, 66; on Web and software resources, 66–67

Responsibilities, 6–8

Rhem, J., 10, 12, 33

Rich text format (RTF), 23

Rocheleau, J., 34

Rose, W., 85

RTF. *See* Rich text format

S

Sacken, M., 51

Safety, 91

Saint Louis University, 49, 53, 80

Saltzberg, S., 31

Schmier, L., 49

Schroeder, L., 81

Schuh, J. H., 10, 11, 25

Second Life, 31

Seldin, P., 6

Self-assessment, 17

Self-evaluation, 95–97

Self-referral effect, 12

"Seven Principles for Good Practice in Undergraduate Education" (Chickering and Gamson), 9, 45

SGID. *See* Small-group instructional diagnosis

Shadiow, L., 66

Shaner, M., 49

Sheppard, L., 110

Shulman, L. S., 15

Sikos, L., 65

Silberman, M., 28–29

Slomianko, J., 32

Small-group instructional diagnosis (SGID), 37

Smallwood, R., 10

Smith, K., 41–42, 60, 67, 80

Smith, R. M., 23

Software resources, 66–67

Speck, B. W., 34

Spurgin, K. M., 87

St. Lawrence University, 50, 52, 72, 79, 95

Stalcup, K. A., 23

Statements of civility, 7

Statistical power analysis, 66

Stephens, J., 34

Strauss, W., 2

Streck, P., 19

Student differences, suggested reading, 116–118

Student information form, 43–44; example 1, 43–44

Students: acquainting, with logistics of course, 27; connection between, and instructor, 25–26, 45; cooperation among, 45–46; letter to, 44–49; preparing, 3–4

Surface learning, 12

Svinicki, M. D., 22, 33

Sweden, 12

Sweeney, R. T., 2

Syllabus: content, 21–22; form, 22–23; functions, 25–34; online, 23–25; online resources for construction of, 118

Syracuse University, 63, 64

T

Table of contents, example, 40–41

Tagg, J., 1, 22, 33

"Taxonomy of Significant Learning" (Fink), 92

Teaching Goals Inventory (Angelo and Cross), 10–11

Teaching philosophy statement, 44–49; example 1, 45–46; example 2, 46–48; example 3, 47–49

Teaching portfolios, suggested reading, 118–119

Teaching, scholarly reflection about, 15–16

Technology, 30–31

Texas A&M University, 73, 90

Texas Christian University, 41, 51

Thacher, P., 52, 95

Time on task, and good practice, 46

Tracey, K., 31

Turner, P., 53

U

Ullmann, W., 63

United States Air Force Academy, 54, 88

United States Code, 20

United States Copyright Office, 20

University of Central Florida, 88, 105, 110

University of Colorado, Bolder, 65

University of Massachusetts, Amherst, 43, 47, 59

University of Minnesota, 42, 60, 67, 80

University of Missouri, St. Louis, 43, 86, 91, 98, 105

University of Nevada, Reno, 84, 110

University of North Carolina, Chapel Hill, 71, 87, 107

V

Valdosta State University (Georgia), 49
Valuing, 14
VARK questionnaire, 110
Vasquez, T., 71
Voller, V., 41–42

W

WebCampus, 22, 26, 27, 35
WebCT, 66–67
Weimer, M., 2, 5, 36, 37, 99
Westrick, S. C., 62
Whitt, E. J., 10, 11, 25
Wiggins, G., 14, 18
Wilhite, M. S., 23

Williams, D. A., 2
Windham, C., 31
Wireless technologies, in class, 86–87
Wlodkowski, R. J., 17, 36, 37
WordPerfect, 23, 24
Worrall, P., 31
Wulff, D. H., 37

Y

YouTube, 31

Z

Zhao, C., 8
Zubizarreta, J., 57, 90